FELICITAS D. GOODMAN, an internationally accredited translator and interpreter, is an assistant professor of anthropology at Denison University. A native of Budapest, Hungary, she is the author of a number of papers on glossolalia, and a volume of satiric fairy tales on the subject of tyranny, *Die Blaue Brücke*.

SPEAKING
IN TONGUES

Speaking in tongues

Felicitas D. Goodman

SPEAKING IN TONGUES

A Cross-Cultural Study of Glossolalia

THE UNIVERSITY OF CHICAGO PRESS

Chicago and London

To Hellmut Wohlenberg (1893–1939), teacher and friend

The University of Chicago Press, Chicago 60637
The University of Chicago Press, Ltd., London
© 1972 by The University of Chicago
All rights reserved. Published 1972
Printed in the United States of America
International Standard Book Number: 0–226–30324–1
Library of Congress Catalog Card Number: 70–182871

Contents

3/2/73
Deg

BL
54
.G64

Preface

At some point during our education, many of us, I am sure, have had the exhilarating experience of encountering an inspiring teacher who had just those answers that gave meaning to some lengthy search and whose questions, hypotheses, and insights all of a sudden made the pieces of a puzzle fall into place. I was such a fortunate student. Reading in folklore and religious behavior, I had continually come up against one obviously quite central pattern to which I could find no key. There were, to mention just a few examples, Hungarian *táltosok* (shamans), men of magic powers, who would lie down, close their eyes, start trembling, and then, "hiding," would start speaking of lost objects, of reasons for illness or misfortune, or of the future. There was the Tibetan state oracle who with closed eyes and flushed face, saliva dripping on his ornate robes, would shout of the events to come for the priestly realm; and there were Amerindian medicine men whose incoherent babblings were received with reverence while the white men watching shook their heads and spoke of hysterical savages. And finally, there was Saint Paul, who saw a great light on his way to Damascus and wrote to the Corinthians about prayer in the language of angels that no one could comprehend. What were these men doing? Did this behavior perhaps have some common source? Did there exist, back in history, some mysterious capacity that was now lost? Or was it still available today?

As far as I could see, most of this perplexing behavior centered around religious or quasireligious concerns. When

I went back to school to earn a master's degree in linguistics after many years of professional work as a multilingual scientific translator, I happened to see an announcement of an anthropology course, "Religion in Native Societies." Perhaps to find some respite from very technical linguistic courses, but mainly impelled by questions about religious behavior that had never ceased to interest me, I enrolled in the course. The lecturer was Erika Bourguignon. Working on her project, becoming familiar with her theoretical framework, and doing research under her guidance became the single most important experience of my graduate-school training and eventually provided the impetus for the investigation of which the present monograph is a report.

Dr. Bourguignon's project concerned just that aspect of religious behavior that had always most fascinated me. What I had perceived in a thousand different fragments, she subsumed under one generalized heading: in a behavior representing the focal point of an entire aura of cultural configurations, some persons, with the aid of various techniques, withdrew, as it were, into an inner space—dissociated themselves from the ordinary reality surrounding them in everyday life. The title of the project was derived from this insight: "A Cross-Cultural Study of Dissociational States."[1] It was initiated by Dr. Bourguignon in June 1963, with the cooperation of Professors Louanna Pettay, now of Sacramento State College, and Adolf Haas, of The Ohio State University Departments of Psychiatry and Internal Medicine, and was supported by grant MH 07463 from the National Institute of Mental Health (Bourguignon 1968b:-ii). I became associated with this project, first as a multilingual translator and then as a research assistant. Through this work, I learned to understand that mental states of dissociation in the above sense, i.e., as a withdrawal from external stimuli, represent a widely distributed human be-

[1] There is an extensive literature on dissociation. Field (1960:19) defines it as a "mental mechanism whereby a split-off part of the personality temporarily possesses the entire field of consciousness and behavior."

havior pattern manifested to a greater or lesser extent by many individuals and varying in incidence from society to society. Readers interested in these distributional studies may wish to consult Bourguignon (1968c).

In the voluminous literature I became acquainted with on the project, I came to see how in many societies the mental state of dissociation could serve as the environment of some other activities: dance, drama, singing. While in this state, people might fall into catatoniclike states, some saw visions, others talked. As a trained linguist, I was more and more drawn to the latter behavior. On the project, we possessed some taped utterances made by people while in a state of dissociation. This type of vocalization is termed *glossolalia* (from Greek *glōssa* tongue, foreign word, and Greek *lalia* speech). When in March 1968 Dr. Bourguignon suggested that I try a study of glossolalia, it was these tapes that represented my initial "raw data." Other data were derived from subsequent fieldwork, begun in June 1968 and continued, with interruptions, until the present.

The theoretical underpinnings of the present research have been brought together from a number of fields. My anthropological training acquainted me with the relevant areas of religious behavior, with ethnopsychiatry, culture change, and peasant culture. Since glossolalia is an act of vocalization, it proved important that I should be familiar with modern linguistics, especially articulatory phonetics, as well as with the thinking of such linguists as Lenneberg, Hockett, and Chomsky.

As mentioned before, most observers reporting on incidences of glossolalia noted that the person uttering such vocalization behaved differently than he did in ordinary circumstances. Some authors used the term trance, others spoke of hysteria, frenzy, ecstasy, madness, when describing this altered mental state of the speaker. This suggested the need for acquiring some knowledge of the fundamentals of neurophysiology. In addition, I derived a deepened understanding of mental states from Fischer's work on drug-induced model psychoses. The research of such men as Hess,

Kleitman, and Koella on yet another dissociative mental state, namely sleep and its concomitant, dreaming, provided a valuable basis for a comparison of data.[2]

Finally, current research journals provided some data on what happened on the biochemical level when people fasted, hyperventilated, and so on, in preparation for achieving dissociation.

To the various authors mentioned above, and to the others referred to further on, I wish to express my indebtedness, as well as to Professors Erika Bourguignon, Roland Fischer, Michael A. Little, Stephen Morris, Henry Schwarz III, and Irving I. Zaretsky, for reading the manuscript and making valuable suggestions.

At this point, it would be delightful for me to trace the steps of discovery along its tortuous path. But this would entail a great deal of repetitious presentation, as tiresome for the reader as for the writer. Fieldwork, as every anthropologist knows, yields its gifts helter-skelter, a spot of light here, a tantalizing new avenue there, and it is the task—and let us admit, the passion—of the researcher to provide order and intellectual linkage. This then I have attempted to do.

In my presentation, I have thought mainly of a fellow anthropologist as reader. Nevertheless, perhaps also the researcher interested in religious behavior and the sociologist perplexed by the contemporary scene at home might find something worthwhile in the following pages. Finally, I hope to have answered, more fully than can be done in the classroom, some of the searching questions put to me by my students. With their lively interest, they have been my silent partners through much of my search.

One last note. At the conclusion of the orals of my Ph.D. generals, the graduate examiner suggested, only half in jest, that perhaps I had found some common features in glos-

---

[2] Sleep and drug-induced experiences including alcohol intoxication have here been considered models of altered states only with respect to their "dissociative" character in the above sense; points of agreement will be mentioned further on; an in-depth, phase-by-phase comparison was not within the scope of the present investigation.

solalia in so many different cultures because the same Holy Spirit was speaking through these people. I submitted that the answer to this remark depended on the belief system, the theology of the addressee. But I very much hope that in addition to presenting some scientific results, modest as they may be, I will be able to convey a little of my wonder at and my reverence for the miracle that is man, which remains awesome whether we postulate a Holy Spirit or not.

Acknowledgments

The research for this book was begun as a part of a larger study, which was supported in whole by Public Health Grant MH 07463 from the National Institute of Mental Health. The project, entitled "Cross-Cultural Study of Dissociational States," was under the direction of Dr. Erika Bourguignon, of the Department of Anthropology, The Ohio State University. To Professor Bourguignon, who suggested the present topic, I should like to express my most grateful appreciation for her continued guidance and for her many helpful hints and suggestions. From Professor Roland Fischer, of the Department of Psychiatry, Division of the Behavioral Sciences, of The Ohio State University College of Medicine, and from Professor Donald R. Meyer, of the Department of Psychology, and from the members of the Department of Linguistics I received valuable training and inspiration. My deepest gratitude is understandably reserved for my many informants, the ministers and the congregation members of the Apostolic churches of Yucatán, for Pastor Domingo Torres Alvarado and his congregation of the Cuarta Iglesia Apostólica of Mexico City, and the Reverend Frank M. Munsey and the congregation of the Evangelical Temple in Hammond, Indiana. I am also very grateful for the financial help I received from the Denison University Research Foundation in the form of a generous award, and for a grant-in-aid for research from the Society of the Sigma Xi.

Some sections of this book appeared in somewhat different

form as articles in the following journals and are here reproduced by the express permission of the publishers:

Karger (Basel) for "Glossolalia: speaking in tongues in four cultural settings," in *Confinia Psychiatrica* 12 (1969) 113–29, and "Glossolalia and single-limb trance: some parallels," in *Psychotherapy and Psychosomatics* 19 (1971) 92–103.

The Society for the Scientific Study of Religion (Philadelphia) for "Phonetic analysis of glossolalia in four cultural settings," in *Journal for the Scientific Study of Religion* 8 (1969) 227–39.

Mouton (The Hague) for "The acquisition of glossolalia behavior," in *Semiotica* 3 (1971) 77–82.

Introduction: The Literature

The literature on glossolalia is relatively scant. It also reflects the absence of any kind of working definition, and too often richness of invention substitutes for careful observation. In some general reviews (Eliade 1951; May 1956), sacerdotal languages with their reverently preserved archaic vocabulary are placed under the same heading as games with nonsense syllables; inarticulate sounds, whistling, and the imitation of animal calls are classed with intellectual exercises such as invented languages and skat songs; ritually employed vocal tricks such as ventriloquism are ranked with spirit possession, which is not the phenomenon of vocalization itself but one of its interpretations within certain cultures, and with hysteria, which is a view of the same behavior from a Western, psychiatric bias, or with xenoglossia, which is another kind of interpretation, namely that the vocalization is some unknown, but natural, intelligible language. And all of this is ultimately subsumed under the rubric glossolalia.

My own colleagues, the ethnographers, have not provided us with a single monograph on the subject. They do occasionally give tantalizing hints about the presence of the behavior, sometimes interpretations of it without bothering to let us know whether the opinions voiced are those of their informants or their own. Rare indeed is the ethnographer who has that quality of detachment that makes it possible for him to report puzzling behavior in such a way that scientific insights, perhaps gained much later, can be successfully applied to its interpretation. Malinowski was one of these outstanding observers. He tells, for instance, of the Trobriand Islanders,

> A slightly different form of communication with spirits is that of the men who have short fits, in which they talk to the *baloma* [spirits of the dead in the Trobriand Islands]. . . . One morning I heard loud and, it seemed to me, quarrelsome vociferation from the other side of the village, and . . . inquired from the natives in my hut what it was. They replied that Gumguya'u—a respectable and quiet man—was talking to the *baloma*. I hurried to the spot, but, arriving too late, found the man exhausted on his bed, apparently asleep. The incident did not arouse any excitement, because, as they said, it has his habit to talk to the *baloma*. The conversation was carried on by Gumguya'u in a loud and high-pitched tone . . . and [had] reference to a big ceremonial boat race which had taken place two days before. . . . The *baloma* [were] expressing their strong disapproval of the meager character of the *sagali* (ceremonial distribution of food) [on that occasion] [1916:165].

We shall come back to this passage to show what the understanding arrived at by the present investigation is able to say as explanation of the conversation with the Trobriand *baloma* (see p. 160).

Instead of being of the quality of the above passage, quite a bit of ethnographic material, especially of the first half of this century, is similar to the following description: "As to the absurd nonsense talked by mediums when they are *urua* or 'possessed' by their familiar demons or spirits, such matter is scarce worth recording, as it appears to be, in most cases, meaningless gibberish" [Best 1925:1070].

Largely ignorant of the ethnographic literature, the majority of the authors of Christian theological discussions are convinced of the uniqueness of the behavior in the Christian church. As Cutten points out, "Speaking with tongues is an experience which most people believe to be confined to apostolic times and bestowed as a special favor on a few followers of the crucified Jesus" [1927:1].

Some theories put forth by these authors seem downright quaint. God gave the primitive church the gift of glossolalia so that foreign languages could be learned rapidly:

> La glossolalia era una habilidad otorgada de Dios para aprender idiomas con rapidez. Era un talento, como el musical o artístico, pero dispensado en forma sobrenatural por el Espíritu para el propósito de predicar el evangelio a los estranjeros [Brumback 1960:51–52].[1]

Or: low-class people engaging in glossolalia have a qualitatively different nervous system than cultured persons presumably not prone to such behavior:

> Persons given to such reactions as those being discussed [glossolalia and various kinetic manifestations occurring during dissociation] are nearly always the ignorant, in whom the lower brain centers and spinal ganglia are relatively strong and the rational and volitional powers residing in the higher centers of the cortex are relatively weak [Clark 1949:97].

One of the most disturbing aspects of the discussions on glossolalia is the recurrent claim that one is dealing with a manifestation of mental illness. Once one has classed something as "abnormal" ("sick"), he can safely put it out of his mind and let the psychiatrist worry about it. "There is reason to believe that present day glossolalia is an abnormal psychological occurrence," Burdick says (1969:75). In psychologically oriented presentations, persons evidencing glossolalia behavior are thus often called schizophrenics, epileptics, or hysterics (Sargant 1957:105), all suggesting the presence of mental derangement. As Lévi-Strauss comments with such keen insight (when speaking about totemism and drawing a parallel to hysteria),

---

1 "Glossolalia was an ability given by God for learning languages rapidly. It was a talent, such as that for music or art, but dispensed supernaturally by the Holy Spirit so that the Gospel could be preached to foreigners."

> The vogue of hysteria demonstrated ... a tendency,
> common to many branches of learning toward the
> close of the nineteenth century, to mark off certain
> human phenomena as though they constituted a
> natural entity—which scholars preferred to regard as
> alien to their own moral universe, thus protecting the
> attachment which they felt toward the latter [1963:1].

This, in a nutshell, can be said to have happened to glossolalia. It was marked off as a natural entity, preferably as alien to the rational, scientific, sober researcher who, all too often, if he had to touch the subject at all, did so with marked signs of disgust.

In the decade of the sixties, interest in glossolalia increased, mainly due to an upsurge of the behavior outside of the Pentecostal movement in various main-line denominations. The result was a number of publications ranging from the journalistic to the theological, anthropological, and psychiatric approach.

Journalistic. Sherrill (1964) in an often-quoted book reviews the history of Pentecostalism, which originated from the American Holiness movement and rediscovered and institutionalized "speaking in tongues." He brings together accounts of hallucinatory experiences, instances of glossolalia interpreted as a natural language, and descriptions of people praying in tongues. All of this is quite effectively strung along on his own encounter with glossolalia, beginning characteristically with his hallucinatory experience of seeing a light and ending with himself speaking in tongues. Gauged by the case histories I was able to gather in the field as well as my data from participant-observation, his report, as far as his own experiences are concerned, is completely accurate. No theoretical framework can be expected within this genre, of course, and none is attempted. What stands out when viewed from my own vantage point is that experiences such as seeing light, involuntary vocalization, euphoria, weeping, and so on, although gathered within the framework of a single report, still are not recognized as deriving from the same, common substratum, namely that of a particular dissociative mental state, an altered state of consciousness. Sherrill in this case is within the Christian tradition, where the gift of tongues, of tears, of interpretation, of prophecy, are considered separate entities instead of manifestations of a single state, as indicated by the present investigation.[2]

Theological. A group of professors from the Southern Baptist Theological Seminary (Stagg et al. 1967) gives a historical view of tongue-speaking within the Christian church, basically as a contribution to the recurrent debate (continuing to date) on whether this behavior should be encouraged, condoned, or forbidden in the Christian worship service. The opinion of the authors is that while, through history, glossolalia has done no harm to the church, neither has it been of any particular value. In the socio-psychological section of the book no attempt at all is made to look at the glossolalist just outside the seminary doors. Instead, there is some speculation on the temper of the time, which represses some individuals and causes them to "erupt into turbulent upheavals." The pastor is enjoined to anticipate the problems of his parishioners and to provide alternate possibilities for them to express their "deeper feelings." This section of the book is a telling commentary

---

[2] The view of ecstatic states as being a gift—implying worth, a manifestation of divine grace—is repeatedly expressed in the Bible. "But you shall receive power when the Holy Spirit has come upon you" (RSV. Acts 1:8). "When the day of Penetcost had come, they were all together in one place. And suddenly a sound came from heaven like the rush of a mighty wind, and it filled all the house where they were sitting. And there appeared to them tongues as of fire, distributed and resting on each one of them. And they were all filled with the Holy Spirit and began to speak in other tongues, as the Spirit gave them utterance" (RSV. Acts 2:1–4). And Paul explains, "Now there are varieties of gifts, but the same Spirit; . . . To one is given through the Spirit the utterance of wisdom, and to another the utterance of knowledge according to the same Spirit, to another faith by the same Spirit, to another gifts of healing by the one Spirit, to another the working of miracles, to another prophecy, to another the ability to distinguish between spirits, to another various kinds of tongues, to another the interpretation of tongues" (RSV. 1 Corinthians 12:4; 8–10).

on how little some theologians are aware of the tools
proffered to them by sociologists, anthropologists, and
psychologists. The professors are talking about behavior
without even scrutinizing it and certainly without analyzing
its various aspects with whatever tools modern social and
behavioral science has available for them.

Anthropological. Hine, in an article published in 1969,
shows effectively what can be done by applying a cross-
cultural approach to the study of glossolalia. She reports
on an anthropological investigation of the Pentecostal
movement in the United States, Mexico, Haiti, and Colombia, combining the use of case histories, questionnaires,
interviews, and participant-observation. By using a functional approach in analyzing the data, she demonstrates
that glossolalia may be a component in the process of commitment to a movement with implications for both personal
and social change. About glossolalia specifically, she says
that it is *sometimes* associated with an altered mental state.
My research leads me to different conclusions. The difference
may be due to the fact that the research group for which
she acts as spokesman (from the Department of Anthropology, University of Minnesota, under the direction of
Dr. Luther Gerlach) has apparently not supplemented its
data on a diachronic level, thus missing some diagnostic
signals of attrition of the glossolalia behavior on the individual level, which can only be explained if we stipulate
that glossolalia is *always* associated with an altered mental
state. Cross-cultural linguistic analysis bears out the same
point. Both of these questions will be taken up in detail
later (pp. 116–23).

Psychiatric. In an article that I unfortunately did not
read until after I had completed the first section of my
fieldwork and had submitted my initial report for publica-
tion (1969b), Spoerri (1967) discusses ecstatic speech, which
he considers the superordinate category, reserving the term
glossolalia for the ritualized, Christian speaking in tongues.
The "speech profile" he shows to be a composite of various
individual qualities; speech has both a horizontal and a

vertical integration, with disturbances possible in either direction. On the basis of case histories, he demonstrates how disintegration of the speech profile may arise in cases of exorcism, acute catatonic schizophrenia, and chronic schizophrenic defects. In the special case of Pentecostal tongue-speaking (which he analyzes on the basis of some tape recordings), he finds a striking resemblance in the utterances with respect to sound formation, vocal color, rhythm, and speech melody. He feels that for further research it would be important to compare the glossolalias of persons speaking different languages. Here then is a very satisfactory dovetailing between two research efforts, independently conceived and separately carried out by scientists from two different fields, Spoerri from psychiatry, myself from linguistics and anthropology. And what he had thought of as a necessary continuation of the research effort, I had already carried out.

Glossolalia is not ordinary, everyday behavior. In fact, as the present investigation will demonstrate, it is associated with altered states of consciousness. This has led some authors to class it as psychotic. Thus Mackie (1921) speaks of the "gift of tongues" as a pathological aspect of Christianity; Cutten (1927), extensively quoted through the years, contends that glossolalia is linked to schizophrenia and hysteria. Modern research, however, has shown significant differences between individuals suffering from mental disorders and individuals participating in religious activities involving glossolalia and other dissociative behavior. Kiev (1964), to name only one, compared ten West Indian schizophrenic patients with clinically normal West Indian Pentecostals and found that the schizophrenic patients could not limit their abnormal behavior to one social context. Thus they were unable to maintain sufficient control of autistic and repressive behavior to fit into the prescribed ritual patterns. Other investigations involving the mental health of Pentecostal groups will be mentioned later (see p. 25).

The problem boils down to the question of whether

altered states *per se* are to be considered pathological. Ludwig (1968) in his review of these mental states carefully avoids this "pathology model" and does not attempt any kind of classification of altered states as being either pathological or nonpathological. This view coincides with the stand taken by many anthropologists. Wallace (1961, 1966, 1970) sees altered mental states as the normal individual's response to stress, leading to a "mazeway resynthesis." La Barre (1970, 1971) similarly views the crisis cults that are associated with these mental states as adaptive mechanisms. And Prince (1968) points out that, in many cultures, the emotionally disturbed are directed by their healer-priest to join possession cults in order to be healed—in recognition of the psychotherapeutic property of dissociative behavior (interpreted as spirit possession; see p. 18).

As my own contribution to this dialogue on glossolalia, I do not want to support or refute any of the above theories on the etiology or the nature of glossolalia and altered states generally. Rather, I should like to offer a description of glossolalia behavior. In this sense, the presentation is within the bounds of ethnographic tradition.

SPEAKING
IN TONGUES

1 The Data:
Settings and Field Experience

We have touched on the question of why I came to be interested in glossolalia, how this behavior is represented in some of the literature, and what the sources were that offered help in solving a few of the problems posed by the research. We are now ready for a closer view of the material we have set out to examine. The logical first questions seem to be: where did I derive this body of data, and how was it obtained?

As mentioned earlier, my initial "raw data" were simply tapes available at Professor Bourguignon's project. Three of the groups represented on these tapes spoke English: a Streams of Power congregation, a tent revival, and a main-line Protestant congregation. The Umbanda tape came from Portuguese-speaking Brazil. In each of these instances the primary objective of the recording was not the glossolalia; the tapes contain only a limited number of samples, and questions concerning, for example, the identity of the speaker, kinetic behavior, physical correlates, and so on, remain largely unanswered.

The following is a brief characterization of these four settings:

Streams of Power. The following information is summarized from Henney (1968), who also made the tape recordings of the glossolalia utterances used for this study.

The Streams of Power movement came to the Caribbean island of Saint Vincent in 1965. It was started in Holland about 1952 and has since spread to the Dutch West Indies and Dutch Guiana and to Trinidad, and Saint Lucia in addi-

tion to Saint Vincent; it derives its membership from the
lower social strata. The congregation is largely composed
of women; about 20 percent are men, another 20 percent
are children. The service usually lasts for two hours. A
period of singing, taking about forty minutes, begins each
service. This singing is loud and fast, and there is much
hand-clapping, stamping of feet, and gesturing. This is
followed by the "Service of Adoration" during which glossolalia is a prominent feature. The evangelist, with his head
elevated and his eyes tightly closed, begins whispering repeatedly into the microphone such phrases as "Thank you,
Jesus," Hallelujah," or "Praise the Lord," setting the pattern for the congregation to do the same. Periodically, someone in the congregation breaks in with a glossolalia utterance, usually concluding with "So speaks the Lord," and
then proceeding in ordinary language with the interpretation.[1] About seven or eight people of both sexes may make
contributions of this nature, including, occasionally, the
evangelist. The latter then closes the Service of Adoration
with prayer.

The glossolalia is viewed by the Streams of Power move-

[1] In a number of denominations practicing tongue-speaking, a
vernacular utterance called "interpretation" follows the true, i.e.,
unintelligible, glossolalia. This is viewed as another one of the gifts of
the Holy Spirit. (See RSV. 1 Cor. 12:10, "to another the interpretation
of tongues.") At the time of this investigation, the congregations of
the Apostolic branch of the Mexican Penetcostal movement did not
practice interpretation. For this reason, the behavior is not discussed
here. Briefly anticipating some insights detailed later (pp. 146–47), as
well as results obtained in other congregations, the "interpretation"
does not represent an explanation or translation of the meaning of the
preceding unintelligible utterance. Rather, the speaker "switches" from
the state producing the glossolalia to one where intelligible speech is
available to him while he still remains in a light trance. He then elabor-
ates memory content on this level. Such utterances, however, still bear
some of the earmarks of true glossolalia. The throat muscles continue
to appear rather tense, the phrases are strongly rhythmical and tend
to be of approximately equal length. In addition, grammar and co-
herence of thought are often neglected. Figure 8 (p. 110), while exhibiting
the very high energy content of true glossolalia, also presents some of
these features.

ment as revealing the words of Jesus himself, or of the Holy Spirit. The message is given in a foreign tongue, and it is its essence that is thought to be subsequently repeated in the vernacular. The unknown tongue is believed to be an ordinary foreign language that could be understood if someone who knew that language happened to be present. The interpretation also rests with the Spirit. According to the evangelist, the person who is speaking "doesn't even know what he is saying."

Speaking in tongues is regarded as a highly desirable "gift of the Spirit" that is accessible to anyone who is a "child of God" (i.e., who has repented). The evangelist emphasizes that speaking in tongues makes a believer strong and guarantees that he will not backslide. The members who speak in tongues state that they feel "uplifted" or "exalted" afterward; it makes them "feel good." They say that they remember speaking in tongues, but do not remember what they said. The altered state manifested in glossolalia is short. Eyes are kept closed; only occasionally is trembling or shaking noted, and it is minimal. Waking is always rapid.

Midwestern Tent Revival. The tape of this tent revival meeting, in the summer of 1966 in Columbus, Ohio, was produced by Linda Kimball, a graduate student at the time in the Department of Anthropology of The Ohio State University. The description of the cultural setting is based on her personal communication.

Tent revivals were brought to this country by immigrants from the English lower working class, and lower-class whites still constitute the bulk of the participants, with only 10 to 30 percent Negroes; 50 to 75 percent of the participants are usually women. As a rule the evangelists are not affiliated with any established church, and there is a great deal of individual variation between them in the way in which they conduct the revival meetings.

The services are only minimally structured. Roughly, three phases can be distinguished: 1) a warm-up period, with a great deal of singing, hand-clapping, and some talking by the assistants of the evangelists; 2*a*) the first excitation period, when the evangelist comes in, gives a sermon, intermingled with singing and possibly some glossolalia; then the offering is taken up, at which time people tend to be quite restless; 2*b*) the second excitation period, when the people feel relaxed, high excitement sets in, there is healing, preaching, trancing, occasionally also glossolalia, and singing; and finally 3) the "cooling-off" period, with singing and hand-clapping, usually in the absence of the evangelist.

Dissociation in this cultural setting is interpreted as the Holy Ghost being *in* the person, as "getting" the Holy Ghost, and as evidence that the person is "right with God." It brings prestige within the group and is considered an enjoyable experience. Glossolalia, according to the preacher, is a sign that the Holy Ghost is "moving the tent" (i.e., the congregation) and makes people *witness*. The main thing, however, is that you "fall down," meaning that you go into trance, showing that the Holy Ghost is really in you, that you are "slain of the Spirit." After speaking in tongues, people report "feeling wonderful."

The glossolalia is as little structured as the rest of the behavior; sometimes it is interpreted, sometimes not—at the meeting represented on the tape, for example, one woman interpreted her own glossolalia and that of several others.

Main-line Protestant Church in Texas. In 1965 the National Educational Television Network presented a program entitled "Divine Healing and Speaking in Tongues." As the announcer points out, such "early Christian practices" have spread from the Pentecostal churches (for a history of this movement, see Bloch-Hoell's account, 1964) to the major denominations, and in the Houston, Texas, area can now be found in Baptist, Episcopalian, and Presbyterian churches. In these congregations, Sherrill reports (1964:139), glossolalia is interpreted as evidence of a "baptism in the spirit." Unfortunately, the bulk of the program time is devoted to the opinions of different churchmen and others, and we are not told in which church or denomination the few glossolalia samples were recorded. (Our local NET station has no master list of taped programs, and this information is no longer available.)

Umbanda. The field research on this Brazilian movement was also carried out by a graduate student in the Department of Anthropology of The Ohio State University, Esther Pressel, in São Paolo, Brazil, in 1966–67. The following summary is based on her report (1968).

The Umbanda cult emerged in Brazil in the 1930s. It is a spiritualist religion in the specialized meaning of focusing on spirit mediumship; its major ritual activity involves altered states of consciousness, interpreted as possession by spirits. These spiritual entities diagnose and treat illnesses and help to solve personal problems in public and private sessions. Usually, the mediums are in a very light state of dissociation, but deeper trance also occurs. During the consultation period in the public session, a spirit occasionally is said to possess a member of the audience, causing the individual to shriek and shake violently.

The details of the phonological (sound inventory) and suprasegmental (intonation, accent, etc.) analysis of these tapes will be outlined later (p. 99). We will have to anticipate here that this analysis showed a surprising cross-cultural agreement, an agreement that could not, to my mind, be due to chance. This agreement consisted principally in the fact that the individual utterance, or the identifiable units within the utterance, showed a threshold of onset, a brief rising gradient of intensity, a peak, and a final, often precipitous decay. This pattern appeared even in the one example where seemingly "meaningful" phrases were uttered —most of the glossolalia utterances are not language in this sense, as has been pointed out earlier by such researchers as Samarin (1968) and his student Wolfram (1966). In addition, the utterances exhibited striking similarities in accent patterns and certain phonological features.

The question arose: did these agreements exist because, in spite of considerable cultural diversity, the three groups, namely the Streams of Power, the tent revival, and the mainline Protestant congregations all spoke English? Was there

an agreement between the samples from English speakers
and the Umbandists, speaking Portuguese, because both
English and Portuguese are related Indo-European languages? And would I find the same agreements if I analyzed
the glossolalia utterances coming from speakers of a non-
Indo-European language? If I did, then what produced
this agreement? Was it perhaps the altered state of consciousness that so many observers reported as usually
present when people spoke in tongues? I suspected that the
latter was the case, and I designed my fieldwork to test the
hypothesis that *the glossolalist speaks the way he does because
his speech behavior is modified by the way the body acts in
the particular mental state, often termed trance, into which
he places himself.* In other words, I conceived of the glossolalia utterance as an artifact of a hyperaroused mental
state or, in Chomskyan terms, as the surface structure of a
nonlinguistic deep structure, that of the altered state of con-
sciouness. This was the inference I proposed to test by a
cross-cultural, cross-linguistic study. In pursuit of this en-
deavor I needed, first of all, to record glossolalia from a
group that spoke a language other than English or Portuguese. For this, to save time and effort, it seemed advisable
to seek out a congregation where I could be reasonably sure
that speaking in tongues was an accepted part of the life of
the group. Some preliminary inquiry indicated that Mexico
had a well-developed Pentecostal movement. I decided to
try my luck there.

With the Mexico City telephone book as my guide, I was
fortunate enough to make contact, in the summer of 1968,
with Pastor Domingo Torres Alvarado and his congregation, the Cuarta Iglesia Apostólica de la fe en Cristo Jesus
in the Colónia Pro Hogar of the Mexican capital. The
Apostolicos are an offshoot of the Pentecostals, differing
from the latter mainly in their belief in the unity of the
Trinity. I revisited this congregation in the summer of 1969,
and also in 1970, thus adding the dimension of time to the
cross-cultural study I was engaged in.

The first Apostolic congregation of Mexico was founded

in 1914. The initial stimulus came from the United States, but the development of the church in Mexico has been an independent one. In 1964 it had about one thousand ministers working in Mexico and in missions in other Latin American countries (Gaxiola 1964:11).

The congregation that I observed is located in one of the poorer sections of the capital. Of the ninety-odd members, about 60 percent are women, approximately 20 percent men, the rest children. Most of them come from the lower middle class. The majority has been in Mexico City less than ten years.

The service usually begins with a hymn, followed by a short prayer during which the congregation stands and each person speaks his own particular petition in an audible voice. After another hymn, testimonies are asked for. These may be of a very personal nature such as the expression of thankfulness for recovery from an illness or a request for prayers for some undertaking, or merely a biblical text. The pastor reads a text from the Bible, sections from the Acts referring to the first Pentecost or Paul's first letter to the Corinthians being perennial favorites. This concludes with another hymn, followed by a *corito* (a small chorus). The hymns are rather fast and very rhythmical, and are accompanied by hand-clapping, but the *corito* has a faster rhythm, a rousing melody. It is brief, everyone knows it by heart, and it usually has a direct reference to the experience of speaking in tongues, such as "*Dios está aquí . . .*" ("God is present here") or "*Fuego, fuego, fuego es que quiero . . .*" ("Fire, fire, fire is what I want"). Clapping becomes strongly animated at this point, and people begin to go to the altar for the altar call. They kneel down, every person prays his own prayer, some very loudly, often with the music (piano and guitar) continuing for a while.

The altar call concludes upon a signal from the pastor's bell. The length of the altar call is determined by the interaction between pastor and congregation. After about ten minutes (longer at services held especially for "receiving the Holy Spirit"), the collective voice level begins to drop. After consulting his wall clock, the pastor reacts with his bell. This is followed by more Bible reading, which the congregation receives standing at its seat, another hymn, then once more a *corito* and a second altar call. After another hymn, the offering is taken, a prayer is given for the offering, and a lengthy sermon follows. It concludes with a hymn and another prayer.

Glossolalia usually occurs during these altar calls. It is considered a manifestation of the Holy Spirit, a baptism of the Spirit that comes to take up its abode in the person as in a tabernacle. People speaking in tongues but leaving the church or not evidencing Christian behavior are thought by the congregation to be possessed by Satan, but this view is not shared by the ministers. It is not believed that glossolalia represents any particular natural language (only the ministers mention occasionally that someone they have heard might have spoken Latin or Greek), and there is never any interpretation.

Women go into glossolalia much more easily than men, and almost all of them are habitual glossolalists. Of the men, less than half reported having a glossolalia experience. The men have an impressive concomitant kinetic behavior such as lifting arms, shaking the head, a twitching in the face; among the women, the only observed consistent accompanying behavior was crying. Also, the men's glossolalia is loud, while that of the women can barely be heard[2] giving rise to the impression that only the men have a strong "manifestation of the Holy Spirit."

Clapping often seems to induce the trance and also to reestablish it once it has decayed. Waking from it is very fast, and it is followed by an intense feeling of well-being. Once a trance with glossolalia has been achieved, subsequent

---

[2] In 1968, I obtained only some fragments of the women's glossolalia. In 1969, however, while the church was being rebuilt, the services were held in a small meeting room and for lack of space the congregation stayed in its place during altar calls. Most people could not even kneel down. Wedged in among the women, I was able to record several samples.

trance events are initiated with great ease; nevertheless, achieving vocalization for the first time after the state of dissociation has been reached seems very difficult for some people.

The above summary is obviously a report of results based on field observations, and this seems to call for a brief discussion of some details of the fieldwork.

In my first interview with Pastor Torres of the Cuarta Iglesia Apostolica I explained that I was working on a university research project, that we were interested in the manifestation of the Holy Spirit termed speaking in tongues, and asked for his permission to join the congregation as an observer. It was with this explanation that he then introduced me to his group. In most ways I conformed to the rules observed by the female members of the church: I wore conservative clothing and went without jewelry and makeup; during services, I sat on the women's side and always covered my head with a mantilla. I stood when they stood, knelt when they knelt, and contributed my offering. That I did not join the singing and clapping, but rather kept writing notes in a small copybook, disturbed no one. After the third meeting, I asked permission to bring a tape recorder, and it was granted as a matter of course. Nor did anyone object to my filming during services the following year.[3] In conver-

---

[3] For sound recording in 1968, I took a tape recorder using 3″ reels to the field. I found the fidelity too poor, although the recorder was handy because of its light weight and relatively small size. Since 1969, I have used a casette tape recorder. I found it very practical to be able to hang it over my shoulder, microphone in hand, and walk in among the kneeling people, holding the microphone very close to the speaker on whom I wanted to focus. Unfortunately, the casettes of the high-quality tapes have open edges; after recording on them, I enclose each one in a separate plastic bag, sealing it with tape as a protection against cockroaches, moisture, and dust. In addition, in 1970, I used a tape recorder with 5″ reels and having a built-in microphone. It has fine fidelity, but for the tiny space I had to work in, in a small, crowded church, it was somewhat too large and its weight made it cumbersome. Under pressure, as I often was, the tape took too long to thread, and in the dim light I could not always be sure what side I was recording on.

sations with the women members I explained that I was a
teacher on vacation and that I was planning to write a book
about the life of the congregation. Our relationship was
soon very friendly; later, when I asked for conversion stories,
they supplied them in great detail. Toward the end of my
first summer's stay with the congregation I wanted to make
a statistical survey, asking for such information as age, oc-
cupation, date of the first glossolalia experience, and so on.
I hesitated for quite a while before I ventured into this, for
fear the members of the congregation might consider these
questions as invasions of their privacy. I need not have been
so shy: one of the young women, when I had completed
her questionnaire, said in a disappointed voice, "¿Es todo?"
—Is that all you want to know?

Only once was I asked, and then by a man, what kind of
language I thought the tongues were. Since I had expected
this question, I was prepared with an answer that would be
considerate of the religious sensitivities of the inquirer while
not violating my own professional convictions. I quoted
Paul (RSV. I Cor. 14:2), "One who speaks in a tongue
speaks not to men but to God; for no one understands him,
but he utters mysteries in the Spirit." He was satisfied.

An observer cannot, of course, enter any kind of a group
without affecting it in some way. In this congregation, for
instance, I heard no glossolalia during the first few services
I attended, although the pastor maintained that there was
some at every altar call. "How do you know?" "It isn't

For filming I use a small super 8 movie camera. It is so light that
at the same time I can have the tape recorder slung over my shoulder
and film with my right hand, carrying it with me everywhere, even
wading into the ocean with it during a baptism. The film print (in
color) is of good enough quality to be used for classroom purposes.
From fifty color film cartridges expended in two summers' work I
had, after editing, two half-hour films of respectable quality ("Speaking
in Tongues in Yucatán" and "Women and Children in a Maya Village"). The light pack and battery I took with me in 1970 did not
function at all, either due to moisture or because they were damaged
during the trip. But an electric-powered lamp proved usable in the
church, which has an electric outlet.

Spanish," was the matter-of-fact answer. I started asking myself in despair whether I had perhaps come to the wrong congregation. Then a chance remark to one of the young deacons of the church, before the service, stimulated him to tell of his conversion experience. In the course of this conversation I had the opportunity to emphasize my interest in the manifestation of the tongues. In the absence of the pastor that evening, this young man was in charge of the service and, perhaps as a result of the implicit reassurance in our conversation, there was a great deal of glossolalia, his own and that of others, much of it distinct enough above the din of the communal prayer to yield an analyzable sound track. This "open" attitude has persisted ever since. At Pastor Torres's request, I sent him copies of papers about my glossolalia research presented at anthropological meetings and published in scientific journals, and he was quite pleased to see his congregation mentioned.

In considering the relatively easy and relaxed observer-group relationship, we must take into consideration the special character of this big-city congregation. This was a meeting of people with the same ritual concerns, many of them recent arrivals from the rural areas for whom the service they had already known at home was a brief spiritual respite from the exigencies of the harsh life of the city.[4] "Changing one's life," in the biblical sense of "leaving the things of the world behind," was a principle given scant lip service and even less reality. After the service, people scattered, and at least some of them did not live in the same *colónia* (city subdivision). While the difference between the service of the *Apostolicos* and the average Catholic service was striking in terms of intimacy, participation, and concern

[4] Once in the city, even those who are obviously recent arrivals from the villages and farms are not viewed as peasants in an urban society—and do not class themselves as such. Instead, they are intensely involved in learning new, nonpeasant roles. As Pressel (1971) points out for the Umbandists of Brazil, and Lalive d'Epinay (1968) for the Pentecostals of Chile, the psychological stresses of the move from a rural environment to an urban environment often lead people into various cult activities.

of the pastor for his parishioners, there was a tendency to
de-emphasize the speaking in tongues and especially the
"excesses," as Pastor Torres put it, of the kinetic behavior
often accompanying the state of dissociation. The reason
was perhaps the desire to appear more acceptably middle
class, as one church official put it. The subject of the Second
Coming of Christ was rarely touched on. Evangelizing
fervor was minimal, and sin was hardly mentioned. There
was no baptism of new members in the three months of
observation in 1968.

What all this meant for my fieldwork was that I was not
really confronted here by any of the participant-observer
problems usually faced by anthropologists in the collection
of their data. It was in many ways an apprenticeship: I
learned to *hear* glossolalia; I learned to become accus-
tomed to observing and recording every possible nuance of
some rather unusual behavior; I learned to use equipment
effectively and unobtrusively. And, mainly, I learned to
cope with the culture shock of seeing people in dissociation,
by no means easily tolerated at the outset, as this quotation
from my field notes will indicate.

From the start, Juan seems to be driving harder, with
hand-clapping and with occasional loud shouts of address
to God and the Holy Spirit. Then his voice drops for a
phrase or two, and all of a sudden, from the middle range,
he goes into a rising glossolalia utterance, "*siø:, siø:, siø:*[5]
. . ." On the tape, the onset is easily discernible, but
upon hearing, it comes to me as a tremendous surprise:
for the first time, a real glossolalia! Again and again,
Juan recovers his energy level: there is a constant pulsing,
curve after curve. As the realization of the powerful
manifestation breaks upon the people in prayer before
the altar, the trance sweeps through them like a fire. I hear
a man on the left, much less intensely than Juan, but with
the same basic pulse, "*siə, siə . . .*" There is a woman on
the right. Instead of letting her arms hang down as

[5] For identification of the phonetic symbols used in these notations
see p. 103.

the people here do in prayer, she has her hands tightly
pressed together, about breast high, moving them up and
down from the wrist with inimitable rapidity, also saying
something like "*siɔ, siɔ* . . ." Suddenly, Juan jumps up
behind the rostrum, where he has been kneeling up to now.
His knees are slightly bent forward, his body is a bit inclined
toward the back, very rigid, his eyes are closed tightly,
his face appears flushed, extremely tense, but not distorted,
his arms outstretched, his hands clenching and then
opening with the rhythm of the pulses. His alternately
rising and falling voice seems to shake and break us with
its volume and intensity. Then there is a steep decline
in both, his arms drop, his eyes open. He catches my glance
and an expression of total, questioning bewilderment
passes over his face. I remember him saying, "I want to
be silent, but my tongue is locked in place, I hear my
words, but I do not understand them." Then, almost
without having to catch his breath, he passes into language
and kneels down again. I can easily see now why glossolalia
is so universally considered a divine inspiration, a possession
by a supernatural being. There is something incredibly,
brutally elemental about such an outbreak of vocalization,
and at the same time something eerily, frighteningly unreal.

The challenge offered by the next section of my fieldwork
was of quite a different nature. Since I now wanted to test
my hypothesis with speakers of a non-Indo-European language, I asked Pastor Torres to put me in touch, if possible,
with the Apostolic church in Yucatán. Yucatecan Maya is
an American Indian language, not related to the Indo-
European language family to which English and Spanish
belong.[6]

The Apostolic movement began on the Yucatecan Peninsula in 1959 as the result of missionizing work done by
a Mexican evangelist named Oscar Gill from the Apostolic
congregation of Guadalajara. There are today *Apostolicos*
in a number of localities in the states of Tabasco and Cam-

[6] Maya languages are classified as belonging to the Macro-Penutian
language family; they are genetically related to some of the Amerindian
languages of California.

peche and the Territory of Quintana Roo on, or close to, the peninsula. My fieldwork centered in a Maya village named Utzpak[7] not too far from the coast, about a hundred kilometers east of Mérida, the capital of Yucatán.

This community has about five thousand inhabitants (information from the 1970 census was kindly supplied by the vice president of the municipality, Don Vicente Lisama), all but about three hundred of them Catholics. The oldest Protestant church of the community is that of the Presbyterians; others represented are the Baptists and Pentecostals. Most of the people are peasants, working their own corn fields (*milpa*), or as farmhands on the large ranches ringing the community. Utzpak lies just outside the henequen belt, the territory producing the only large cash crop of the peninsula, and is thus less affected by the decline of the significance of this commercially used fiber on the world market. As one of my informants put it, *"En Utzpak, la gente es pobre, pero pobres pobres no hay"*—People are poor in Utzpak, but no one is really starving.

The church is located close to the center of town, in a side street. It was built by the members on a plot given to the congregation as a gift by one of the older *hermanos*. It is a mud-and-wattle structure with a tarpaper roof and wooden shutters for the window openings. It has a cement floor and electricity. The people sit on wooden folding chairs, the women on the left as one comes in, the men on the right. A narrow section in the center is set off for the young people. The altar is a low podium, to which two steps lead up on either side. Its center front is occupied by a rostrum, and in 1970 a public-address system was added, a gift from congregations in the United States. Colored paper garlands are strung over the main section of the church, which is about thirty-five feet long and eighteen feet wide. The rostrum is decorated with a hand-embroidered cloth, and there are two flower vases that are always filled with fresh flowers and aromatic branches. The church has

[7] Not its real name.

a guitar and a *marimbol*, a home-made instrument made of metal strips of different lengths fastened to a wooden body that serves as a resonator. The metal strips are plucked with the thumb. In the back, a man-high wall separates the church from a section that serves as the living quarters for the minister and his family. The church is surrounded by a stone wall and has its own "half well."

When I arrived in Utzpak in June 1969 the congregation was almost dormant, but its restless, dynamic new pastor, who arrived almost at the same time I did, soon breathed vigorous life into it. In fact, in August 1970 when I left after a second summer of observation, this congregation had become one of the breeding grounds for an intense millenary or revitalization movement. That is why, in discussing the community, I am continually involved with the description of change.

Thus, the active membership of the church in June 1969 was about seven men and five women; by the middle of August of the same year it had risen to fifteen men and ten women, and by the end of July 1970 it had increased to more than double that figure. There was a baptism of an unprecedented sixteen new members on 1 August, further swelling the congregation.

The services, although of the same general ceremonial structure as those in Mexico City, also showed some differences. Each service concluded with an extensive prayer for the sick. There was an almost military precision to such ritual occasions as the procession of the various organizations within the church (the men's, the women's, and the young people's society). Mainly, for the fieldworker, they were from the start physically more demanding. There was a great deal more standing, prolonged periods of kneeling (up to one hour or more), and more vigorous clapping. Under the impact of the burgeoning excitement in the latter part of the summer of 1970, some of the ritual structure disintegrated and there was quite a bit of innovation, the most impressive of which consisted in members of the congregation going to the *casa pastoral*, the pastor's house, under the same roof as the church and separated from its main body, as mentioned before, only by a man-high wall, and praying in glossolalia there,[8] not loud enough to disrupt the goings-on in the church but so audible that it provided a dramatically effective accompaniment and counterpoint to the ritual events of the service.

The glossolalia, while always of intense ritual value, became increasingly the focus of attention. Finally, it even acquired a new function, being in the eyes of the congregation the single most effective weapon of exorcism at the time when they were in the throes of a rash of visions and possession experiences: when, during the service preceding the baptism scheduled for the next day, one of the *hermanos* claimed to have become possessed by Satan who demanded the soul of one of the baptismal candidates, an attractive young woman, Satan did not yield to the usually effective formula: "Satanás, en el nombre de Dios te reprendo" ("Satan, in the name of the Lord, I expel you"). He did not relinquish his hold on the *hermano* until Lorenzo,[9] the minister, and some of the other *hermanos* surrounded the

[8] In denominations practicing tongue-speaking, the behavior is interpreted in two ways. First of all, it indicates the presence of the Holy Spirit *in* the person: "They were all filled with the Holy Spirit and began to speak in other tongues, as the Spirit gave them utterance" (RSV. Acts 2:4). In anthropology, this is termed a form of possession belief, although the terminology is not always uniform. As Bourguignon (1968b:2) points out, "In the ethnographic literature, the terms "trance" and "possession" are used widely, inconsistently and often interchangeably. In order to utilize the available materials, we had to admit very broad definitions of our terms, while distinguishing between "trance" as a level of behavior and "possession" as one of native belief or theory about behavior and/or events. . . . When behavior or physical states of human beings were attributed to an agency other than the person himself, but not caused by external action on the person, we admitted the existence of "possession" belief, whatever the native phrasing might be." Secondly, speaking in tongues is viewed as a form of prayer, inspired by the presence of the Holy Spirit. "For one who speaks in a tongue speaks not to men but to God; for no one understands him, but he utters mysteries in the Spirit" (RSV. 1 Cor. 14:2).

[9] All the names of the members of this congregation have been changed to protect the privacy of those concerned.

possessed one and prayed in glossolalia. Satan, deprived of his abode in the *hermano*, thereupon went out into the street in front of the church and had to be dislodged once more, again with a very loud prayer in tongues.

Also, at the beginning of the observation, glossolalia was not interpreted (see n. 1, p. 4). As the fervor of the millenary movement grew, "other gifts of the Holy Spirit also became manifest," among them interpretation. This was not, however, of the general devotional kind, as for instance among the Streams of Power adherents, but rather very specific. It was thought that the Holy Spirit was "using the bodies of the *hermanos* to transmit messages" about such immediately urgent matters as where to send evangelists, how to arrange financial support for them, what preparations to make, since the visions received indicated that the Second Coming was just around the corner.

This then was the congregation that I entered, armed with years of anthropological training, to be sure, but fundamentally basing myself on the experiences I had gathered during fieldwork in Mexico City. I honestly expected no great surprises.

That there would be considerable differences between the work in the metropolitan congregation and one out in the bush village was of course to be anticipated, but I had certainly underestimated its emotional impact on me as a fieldworker. This was brought home to me during the very first service I attended in Maya country. I am quoting from my field notes:

This service takes place in Temax, a village close to Utzpak, in the home of a family, or rather in the yard, for the small, oval, mud-and-wattle apsidal house with its domed, *uano* (palm frond) thatched roof does not have room for even this small a congregation. The table of the family serves as altar. It has an embroidered tablecloth, a plastic dish for the offerings, two green houseplants for decoration. A Coleman lamp is burning on the *albarrada*, a high garden wall of jagged limestone, moths and an enormous tropical cockroach whirring around it.

The congregation at the start consists of twelve women, six men, some children; more people keep coming. In his sermon the minister says that before the Spaniards came, the Mayas worshipped enormous, hideous stone idols. The Catholics brought them a little doll, with a nice face and well painted lips, but all that happened was that people passed from an ugly idol to a pretty one. Then he extols the gifts of the Holy Spirit, such as speaking in tongues, that the Catholics know nothing about. He introduces me (having rehearsed beforehand how to pronounce Columbus, Ohio), and asks me to say something.

There I stand, under the oleander blossoms before a thatched Maya house. The women are in ?*ipiles,* their embroidered folk costume, *rebozos* covering their heads, some young, some old or even very old. One is suckling her babe, another a beggar who happened by, asking for her *caridad* (alms), who has stayed to listen. Some look down on their laps, others turn toward me, their faces as if with shutters down, neither smiling nor frowning. I feel very much the stranger, the intruder; before these silent faces, what is the value of my rather glib, very intellectual approach to their treasure? So I say, rather haltingly, that I bring greetings from *Hermano* Domingo Torres's congregation in the capital. Then I tell how tired the world out there is of wars and other evils, and how it wants to hear of miracles, such as the gift of tongues. I came to learn about it from them, I say, so I can go back and tell about it.

Some of the women nod, there is a "*Gloria a Dios, aleluya*" from a male voice. I ask the pastor later if he thought that they understood me. "*Pues,*" he shrugs, "who knows?" Then he adds, "I told them not to be afraid of you just because you're white."

I was still taking my cue from the Mexico City experience, though. What was useful there should serve here. For instance, I could have done no work whatever in the Cuarta Iglesia had I not spoken Spanish. Although I knew from my readings about Yucatán that the population is largely bilingual (Maya and Spanish), I started learning Maya in the school year preceding the first observation and continued to do so while in Utzpak. I shaped my external life so that it would conform as closely as possible to that of the women in the congregation: I lived with the family of one of the members of the congregation; I ate the same kind of food, slept in a hammock, wore the same clothes, and learned the social conventions. Within the congregation, I once more participated in the services, adjusting to the special practices, while claiming the right for myself to discharge my duties as an observer: to take notes, to use a tape recorder, and to film. Some of these efforts were highly rewarding. Even my most fractured Maya brought delighted responses and increased acceptance from the women of the congregation. As a result of my external adjustments, I was soon so completely identified in the eyes of the community at large with the *Apostolicos* that I even shared in the ostracism by the larger village society that the *hermanos* were subject to. (Protestants of all denominations are shunned in many parts of the intensely Catholic Latin-American world.) What I did not realize at the outset, however, was that within the congregation my role as an observer was on shaky ground. One reason was that there just was no configuration available within this group that would admit such a role. Second, I was increasingly drawn into the vortex of a kind of social change that assumed such momentum that I was at a loss as to how to extricate myself. This congregation progressively conceived of itself as a special community in direct communication with the Holy Spirit, being given messages about the imminent Second Coming. Everyone was to surrender his personal property, all who could were to go out and tell the world of the impending event.

All this I understood only by stages. For instance, the minister introduced me to his congregation as "*hermana* Felicitas." I took this to be a polite formula, nothing more. When I also used the term for various women I came to know who did not, however, belong to the congregation, I was startled by the vehemence of the rejoinder, "*No* es Hermana!"—"She is not a Sister!"—with capital letters. Or: I was taken aback when I heard a prayer uttered for me, telling the Lord that I came, leaving my family behind me, to live with them in poverty and humility so that I would receive the gift of the Holy Spirit in order that I might eventually go back and preach the Gospel to thousands and thousands of souls. I was beginning to learn that my own statements, my behavior, my willingness to be called *Hermana*, were quite logically being interpreted, within the world view of the congregation, as a declaration of intent, which had to lead, inescapably, to ultimate commitment. For this group was, in fact, making a total-life appeal. The Second Coming was close at hand, very close, there could be nothing more important than becoming baptized and then going out to preach to all the souls. Isaía, one of the leading men of the congregation, said during the last, momentous week of my stay with the group (as recorded in my notes):

"God does not want the death of a single sinner."
He breaks into tears, bending over his Bible, then kneels and lapses into a glossolalia prayer, quickly joined by most of the congregation.[10]

My recaltitrant attitude—for this was their interpretation of my insistence on the observer role—was at first the object of loving concern. "If you are not baptized correctly in the name of Jesus Christ, by total immersion in water, and by the Holy Spirit, evidenced by the tongues, how can we meet in the Kingdom of Heaven?" Then in the following year, it led to censure: "You are being very rebellious in the matters of the Lord," which coincided with the older *hermanos* beginning to call me *hermanita* (little sister) used not as an endearment but as a kinship term: younger sister. And finally, at the peak of the upheaval in 1970 (Goodman 1971c), there was a threat of supernatural sanction. "I [the pastor] am impelled by a power to say these things, these are not my words. . . . The Devil is being defeated, so give in to God. . . . You, *Hermana* Felicitas, if you don't surrender to God, you will most certainly die."

10 Unless indicated otherwise, all subsequent quotations are from my field notes.

To respond to these increasing social pressures by refusing to be classed as *hermana* would not have salvaged my status as observer: there was no other explanation admissible within the culture for my continued attendance at the services, for despite all explanations the observer's activities per se were not comprehensible to them. Yet submitting to a baptism and faking glossolalia was no way out either. In the first place, I considered that course of action dishonest; and also, it was potentially dangerous to my usefulness as a fieldworker. As we shall see later, a state of dissociation can be attained very easily, sometimes even inadvertently, and one cannot observe and be dissociated at the same time. Still, I had to find a solution, not only for the sake of the fieldwork I set out to do, but also because as an anthropologist I was duty-bound to leave the field in such a way that a restudy either by me or by someone else would be possible at all times. I finally hit on the only escape route that was both culturally acceptable and left the door open for later visits: I professed that I still had to wait for my husband. As a married woman, I did not want to be baptized alone, and he had "not yet repented." This secured me both a respite and some sympathetic understanding: many women have obstinate husbands.

These then were some of the field conditions under which the research material to be discussed in the following pages was gathered.

2 Conversion Stories

Progressively, in the previous pages, we have moved from the periphery, so to speak, toward the center of our inquiry, which is glossolalia behavior. From answering the question of how the research came to be undertaken and in what way the problem was reflected in the literature, we went on to take a glimpse of the fieldworker as she entered the community in which the behavior of speaking in tongues was to be found. There is one more aspect to concern us before we embark on the core subject: we must consider the *people* who utter glossolalia. Who are these people? And what is it that they experience?

In order to be able to answer these questions, I collected a total of twenty-nine conversion stories. Most of them were recounted to me when the speakers knew me well and did not feel reticent about speaking of their experiences. They were all taped, except for the four testimonies obtained from members of the Hammond, Indiana, congregation (one of whom was from Jamaica), of which no sample is included here. Taping was done either in the church, before or after the service, or in the home. The language of the tapes is either Spanish or Maya. Later, I transcribed the tapes and checked these transcriptions for accuracy with native speakers. The ones included in the sample to follow (ten complete stories plus two sections from additional ones) were then edited in order to make the story line continuous and to cut out repetition. Translation came last. At all times, I tried to preserve the individuality of the speaker.

It should be pointed out here that not one of the twenty-nine informants interviewed appeared to be psychotic. This observation tallies with that of other researchers. Alland (1961), studying a Negro Pentecostal church, found that the practicing glossolalists of the congregation were well adjusted to their social environment and behaved normally except for their tongue-speaking. He calls attention to the fact that the trance states involved cannot be considered an automatic result of personality disorder since, according to his data, the behavior is learned. In another instance, Vivier van Etfeldt (1968), working in South Africa, tested two carefully matched groups, one group made up of members of a church practicing glossolalia, the other group from an orthodox reformed traditional church where the behavior was not accepted. Various tests such as the Thematic Apperception Test (TAT) and the Personality Factor Test of Cattell, with a battery of other tests, indicated that the glossolalist was, for example, less subject to suggestion than his conservative counterpart and also better adjusted. In addition, Vivier van Etfeldt writes, " . . . the tests in this study serve to discount [the possibility of] an inherent weakness in the neural organisation [of glossolalists]" (1968:173). Hine (1969), on the basis of an anthropological study of the Pentecostal movement in the United States, Mexico, Haiti, and Colombia, summarizes the findings of her group by saying, "Quite clearly, available evidence requires that an explanation of glossolalia as pathological be discarded" (217). Garrison (n.d.) similarly found no pathology in glossolalists during a controlled comparison of Puerto Rican Pentecostals and Catholics.

Beyond this aspect, however, and in addition to their fundamentalist convictions about the nature of the "manifestation of the Holy Spirit," the only other trait the informants have in common is a view of a "before and after" phase in their lives: "Before, I was a sinner; now I am saved, and my life is very different" is the ever-recurring theme. As to personality structure, they differ greatly from one another (see Goodman 1971c). This counters the argument that a similarity in personality structure acts as a selective factor for membership in the Pentecostal movement. The people who speak to us in the conversion stories further differ in the reasons *they* give for joining the congregation. (For an analysis of psychological motivations present in a particular group, as interpreted by the observer, see Goodman 1971c). They differ in what they consider important in their experience subsequent to joining the group, and, finally, there is certainly a big difference in the way in which they perceive of the altered state of consciousness and the attendant glossolalia. These differences will be pointed out in conjunction with the conversion stories. It may be interesting to note here that Fischer found the same to be true of the drug experience, as seen in drug-induced (model) psychoses (1968). And elsewhere (1969b:107) he says, " 'Dissociation' between an autonomic function and the perceptual-behavioral variable can be appraised as the resultant of two sequential processes: (1) central nervous activity, . . . and (2) the symbolic interpretation of that arousal." He then continues, "Each experimental subject interprets his central nervous system activity in the light of his total past, that is, the history of his genotype, phenotype, and their interactions between themselves and their environment" (107). The psychiatrist speaks a different language than the anthropologist, but the latter means the same thing when he speaks of the personality structure and cultural conditioning, of which I shall have much to say later, as determining experience.

The ultimate selection of ten, with sections of two more, conversion stories to be presented here was determined by their degree of completeness—due to circumstance, some accounts remained fragmentary—and the skill and introspection of the raconteur. I excluded the four accounts from the Hammond, Indiana, congregation, including the one from Jamaica, because in my fieldwork I had concentrated mainly on Mexico City and Yucatán and thus felt more competent in these areas. Of the ten complete stories given, the first four come from the congregation in Mexico City, one of the largest metropolitan complexes of the Western

Hemisphere. Not one of the informants was born there, and one (Trinidad) does not live there. The other six are from Yucatán, three from urban areas, three from Utzpak.

Although both the Mexico City and the Yucatecan congregations belong to the Apostolic branch of the Pentecostal movement, some differences in dogma seem to be evolving between two areas, of significance for the interpretation of certain aspects of glossolalia behavior. In the Mexico City congregation, sin is rarely mentioned in the sermons. Yet among the parishioners it is thought that transgressions will lead to a loss of the capacity for glossolalia (see the conversion stories of Trinidad and Salvador). This was the first intimation I had that the behavior could be "lost," not only in the sense of the generally encountered belief in loss as a retribution for some offense, but as an actual, perceived attenuation of the capability, for which this belief acted as an interpretation. That this attenuation existed and was most probably neurophysiologically based was to become for me one of the most surprising findings of the diachronic study here reported.

The Yucatecan congregations being of a much more recent date than the Mexico City ones, they have not as yet had to come to grips with the phenomenon of attenuation in glossolalia behavior. Here, a semantically based elaboration of the concept of sin has taken place, again possessing its implications for glossolalia. In Maya, there is no term for sin, only the Spanish loan word *pecado*. This loan word is apparently perceived as semantically empty and in Maya discourse is often avoided by circumlocution. When talking Spanish, Maya speakers, at least those within the Pentecostal movement, use a formulaic enumeration of content—*cine*, *baile*, *tomar*, *fumar*, picture shows, dances, drinking, smoking—to take its place. Engaging in any one of these is thought to make it impossible for a person to receive the baptism of the Holy Spirit, i.e., to start speaking in tongues.

As to the trance and glossolalia experience, various aspects of it become important for the individual informant, while all agree on the joyousness of the experience: the startling perception that one's tongue is no longer amenable to conscious control (Juan); that the behavior can be acquired inadvertently (Trinidad, Salvador), may take hold of him at odd moments later (Trinidad), become lost (Salvador), or cannot easily be shaken off (Maria-Luisa); in addition to altered somatic perceptions (Nohoč Felipe), there may be visual (Salvador, Gregoria) or auditory hallucinations (Chela, Lorenzo); the moment of conversion may be related to the hallucination (Gregoria) or the trance experience (Lorenzo) instead of to the speaking in tongues. The details can be found in the discussions following the individual conversion stories.

1. *Juan.* A professional soldier when he was converted, Juan, unmarried, was very active in the Cuarta Iglesia in Mexico City in the summers of 1968 and 1969, preparing to enter the ministry. He is slender but muscular, in phenotype more Indian than white, friendly and outgoing. His account was taped during the conversation mentioned in Chapter 1.

Juan D. L., Mexico City, Summer 1968

I was converted about four years ago, and I wanted to become a minister. This congregation even sent me to study at the Bible Institute, but for three years I prayed for the manifestation [speaking in tongues], and this manifestation did not come. We here at this church follow the system of, we might say, the first ministers, as described in Matthew 7, that is, that a person, in order to become a minister, must be baptized by the Holy Spirit. Well, then I tempted God in this way. I said, "All right Lord, it seems you want me to become a minister. But those men the Bible talks about were full of the Holy Spirit. So I think I should be full of the Holy Spirit also. So: if you really want me to become a minister, well, then baptize me with the Holy Spirit. But if you won't, well, then I'll know that I am not called for the ministry." I remember this exactly because it was so important for me. It was precisely a year ago this July second that I was praying in that way for the outpouring of the Holy Spirit, and an *hermano* approached me. He was a bishop of our church. He approached me and

laid his hands on my head, and he prayed for me. And
after this *hermano* had prayed for me, I continued praying
alone, beseeching God for this gift. Then it happened
that my tongue became caught, and immediately I knew
nothing, I knew nothing at all, but I did feel this impulse
to speak. I wanted to stop talking, but my tongue was
in this way impulsed. I have noted since then, on other
occasions that I would be praying, and I would insist to
myself that I would not talk, but then I hear my own words,
I don't understand them, but I keep feeling my tongue
pushed to talk.

Afterward I felt strong, and well, and all my problems
were forgotten. It is a blessing, this manifestation. With
it, God comes to live in the Christian, he takes him as a
temple, as a tabernacle. I understand that the Old Testament
speaks of a tabernacle, erected by man, where the Spirit
of God lived, of the Lord Jehovah, or the Lord Jesus,
which is all the same. Today, we are this tabernacle, not
made by the hand of man, but by the will of God. If one
really consecrates his body to God, then I believe that
in the baptism of the Holy Spirit this same God lowers
himself into the person, comes into him, seeks him out
as a temple, as a tabernacle.

There are Christians, on the other hand, who, as we
here say, have fallen from grace, and still have this
manifestation. These manifestations, of course, are not
from God, these are of the Enemy, of the Devil, of Satan,
—this word that one should not mention in polite society,
—[he chuckles] for also the Enemy has his own
manifestation.

Juan, as we see, has obvious difficulties achieving glossolalia: for three years he prays for the manifestation in
vain. We shall come back to why that should be so in this
particular congregation.

He therefore decides to goad God into giving a sign that
indeed he wants him to go into the ministry. Beyond the
quite general expectation within his group, namely that the
Holy Spirit will baptize a person and this will be evidenced
by the gift of tongues, i.e., in the form of a dissociative behavior culminating in vocalization, he adds a powerful

personal motivation and expectation: he very badly wants to become a minister, and thus must show proof of his select status in the eyes of the congregation.

Juan has, of course, often seen people go into dissociation when a pastor prays for them and lays on hands. In his case, the situation has added significance because of the high office of the *hermano* who now so prays for him. When the experience comes, there is first of all the wonder at the physically perceived and perceivable fact that he is no longer able, by his own volition, to manipulate a part of his body, namely his tongue, which here stands for the entire vocal apparatus: *mi lengua se travó*, he says, my tongue was locked in place, it was stuck. Actually, he usually also performs other automatic movements, as we saw in Chapter 2; he jumps up from a kneeling position, he forms a fist, opens his hand again, but he is not aware of this kinetic behavior at all, only of his recalcitrant tongue.

His belief system offers an interpretation: he has no control over his tongue, and yet it performs an act of vocalization, albeit not in intelligible signals—I hear my words, but I do not understand them—because an outside agency has got hold of it. This agency is the Holy Spirit, entering the body that is now a tabernacle, a receptacle. The receptacle, Juan says, can also contain a different kind of supernatural entity, Satan, and this entity can equally avail itself of the speech organs.

On a very personal level, Juan feels that God has now indeed confirmed his call to the ministry in an act of promise directed to him alone. It is obvious that subsequent glossolalia experiences will not have the considerable impact of this first one. One bit of information is given only as a side remark, and that is the date of the experience: 2 July 1967. Its significance will become clear later.

2. *Salvador.* Salvador is a small man in his early forties, rather dark skinned, thinning, black, wavy hair; he walks with a light stoop. Before going into glossolalia, he usually prays with a great deal of movement, lifting both arms, stretching one arm forward, forming a fist, and pounding

the podium serving as altar. This is a generally observed
behavior among the men in this congregation.

Salvador A. Z., Mexico City, Summer 1968

Before knowing anything about the Gospel, I started
attending some services in my home village. Neither did
I know anything about the Holy Spirit. Now, in the small
village, people are not very well informed, not even the
minister. It was only my third time of going to a service,
and I was told that we would pray for two women so that
they would receive the Holy Spirit. I really had no business
praying for them, for I did not have it either yet. But I
did not know this, and so I started praying for them.
And seeing the manifestation of the Holy Spirit in them,
it was given to me that I should sing the praise of the Lord
in tongues, and I sang it for a very long time, and at this
occasion I saw a light that descended from heaven. It was
very beautiful, and a very great joy for me. Never again
did I ever feel the same joy.

I continued going to the services, but I did not again
speak in tongues. At that time my wife and I were not
married, and probably for this reason: what I experienced,
was only a visit by the Lord, and afterward he withdrew
his blessing from me.

When we were already living here in Mexico City,
I brought a relative with me to live with us, and he had
a New Testament with him. He always kept it in his
bedroom. I have always enjoyed reading, but I had never
read the Bible, only some tracts, which I did not understand.

This all happened at a time when I was greatly worried
about work. I used to be a professional soldier, but now
I was working at home as a shoemaker. I was not making
enough to live on, and so I thought I would reenlist.
However, here in Mexico, you can enlist up to the age of
twenty-nine, and from thirty on they don't accept you
any more. I was already thirty-three years old, and so
they would not take me.

Some time went by, and I decided once more that
maybe I should try to enlist anyway, maybe they would
accept me. I went to the office and a man there says,
"I'll try to take care of this for you, but it takes time,
because the papers need to be put in order." Then after

a while, he says, "*Bueno*, I'll try to do it for you faster."
So he went to the typewriter, and he filled out the paper,
but he asked me for no information, that I was already
in the Army once before, six years ago, or about my
discharge. Sure enough, the next day, these papers that
he wrote came back, asking for all the information that
was missing. So I said to him, "*Oigue, mi subteniente*,
how come these other men all bring along their papers,
and I sent nothing along with my form?" He says, "What
you want is to get credit for the time you served, isn't it?"
"No," I say, "what I want is to work, I don't care if they
give me credit for the time I served or that they recognize
my rank." "*Bueno*," he says, "I'll fix you up with another
paper." But, in this paper, all he said was that I wanted
no credit for the time served and that I wanted to work
once more. And I signed it.

The man sent the paper on, but the others in the office
kept telling me that this was of no value, the paper would
do nothing for me since I had signed it myself, and that
it might even get me into trouble.

However, I had read a text in the Bible where it says
that "anything you will ask in my name, believing, you
shall receive." In the beginning, I did not pay much
attention to this text, but I continued reading, and reading.

I went back to the office and I said, "You better tell
me the truth: my problem cannot be taken care of."
"*Pues*, not exactly," he says. So I say to him, "They rejected
me, *¿verdad?* They say that for such and such a reason,
I cannot work here." "No," he says, "all it says here is
that you should talk to the chief of the section. That's
the rule."

So I went back home, and I continued reading, and the
Word of God seemed to make more sense to me now.
So I say to myself, here is an opportunity for me to test
if, truly, God listens and performs miracles. So I go out
to a field, under a tree; there I stop, and I say, "Lord,
if you want me to work, then let it happen in a way that
it should be clear that it was with your help, and I will
follow you. And if you don't want it, then let me have some
sort of sign, so I won't go back to that office and waste
my time. But you know that I need work!"

These were my words, and I understand that they were
not the words of prayer, but they were my words from all
my heart, and directly to God. This I understood.

So I went back and the man says, "So, you again with
your paper." So I said, "Look, let me pass, please, just
let me talk to the chief." So he finally let me pass [from the
waiting room] into the outer office of the chief, and the
top sergeant there was paying no attention, so I went on,
and there were two men standing there, talking, and I said,
"Pardon me, but who is your chief?" And one man said,
"What do you want?" So I told him about my problem,
and he looked at my paper and said, "What you need
is your birth certificate." And I said, "If I had that,
I would bring it, but to get it I would have to travel to
my village, and for that I need money for the ticket.
If I had that money, I would not even be here, but would
rather buy material and continue working, making shoes
at home." "*Bueno*," he says, "and what kind of work did
you apply for here?" "I want to work in hand-to-hand
combat and bayonet use." "That is very good work that
you applied for," he says, "and just for that, I will take
care of your papers this very day, and I'll give you credit
for your time and rank. Come back at twelve."

I felt something very great, and I was very happy, and
at twelve I was back, and wanted to go to the chief again,
but the man said, "Nobody can enter there, but your
papers are already here, all taken care of." And I
understood that this was the work of the Lord, and I felt
God's love when I saw this miracle. Next day, I began
earning, and this is how it was that I began to accept
what the Bible says.

I was baptized in this church here. Unhappily, I began
having fights with my wife again, because she would not
accept the Gospel. You might say I fell into sin, I returned
to vice, to the things of the world. But I kept on praying,
saying, "Please, Lord, look, I started sinning once more
but I do want to feel you close again, as I did once, when
I spoke in tongues." Finally, my wife also was converted.
Upon that, a year ago this 26 June, I once more received
the Holy Spirit at this altar here, and I started speaking
in tongues again. [At this point in his narration, Salvador

stops. A nervous shiver runs over his face, his mouth
twitches, his eyes close: he is trying to suppress an oncoming
glossolalia utterance. He succeeds and continues.] From
then on my life changed. The road of God is pure happiness.
The gift the Holy Spirit gave me is that of speaking
to the souls [preaching]. For instance, yesterday I spoke
with a man who talks in nothing but curse words. God
does not exist for him. But the Holy Spirit gave me the
words to speak to him. So it is great joy to speak in other
tongues, and to preach to the people, full of the Holy
Spirit, as now . . . now . . . [Once more his face twitches,
his lips tremble, his eyes are closed, and he breaks into
a brief utterance. Then his face relaxes, his eyes open
with the words *Gloria al Señor Jesus Cristo*. This is the
manifestation of the Holy Spirit.] With the Holy Spirit,
all is new. However, the Holy Spirit is very sensitive
[*muy delicado*; also: easily offended], and if we do something
bad, it will leave us, and to have it return, that is difficult.

In contrast to Juan, Salvador's aspirations are not involved with the glossolalia experience. Dissociation, as
evidenced by the hallucinatory image of the descending
light, and then glossolalia come to him as he watches the
behavior of the two women;[1] he may have observed others
in the village congregation, but apparently this was out of
awareness. Judging from his report, the hallucination and
the glossolalia seem continuous, they take place within the
same mental state. Although not familiar with the lore
concerning this behavior, he tells of great joy, which is not
repeated in later occurrences. Nor is there any hallucination
connected with the subsequent speaking in tongues.

The behavior pattern is forgotten as easily as it had been
acquired. This is highly disturbing to Salvador: if, by the
interpretation of the congregation, the Holy Spirit granted

[1] A similar occurence is reported in the New Testament: "While
Peter was still saying this, the Holy Spirit fell on all who had heard
the word. And the believers from among the circumcised who had
come with Peter were amazed, because the gift of the Holy Spirit had
been poured out even on the Gentiles. For they heard them speaking
in tongues and extolling God" (RSV. Acts 11:44–46).

him this unexpected boon, why would he then be deprived
of it so promptly? Within the belief system of the group, an
answer is ready, indicating that this must be a frequent
occurrence: he must have committed a transgression, which
now needs to be identified in order for Salvador to be able
to cope with his experience of abandonment. The Holy
Spirit is *muy delicado*, very sensitive, easily offended, and
Salvador was not legally married to his wife at the time he
received the baptism of the Holy Spirit. This social pattern,
sometimes called free union, is very common all over the
Latin American world and is much inveighed against by the
Apostolic church; no one can be baptized until he legalizes
his marital status.

Salvador regained his capacity for speaking in tongues
on 26 June 1967. Juan, we recall, spoke in tongues for the
first time on 2 July of the same year. On 26 June, the Cuarta
Iglesia was host to a singing and evangelizing group from
el otro lado, the other side, i.e., the United States. When I
was in the Mexican congregation in 1968, this visit was still
much discussed. "It was beautiful," said Salvador. "The
Lord manifested himself grandly," was Juan's comment.
"It was miraculous," reported another. "Every one of them
spoke *en otros idiomas* (other tongues)."

Now: Salvador acquired the capacity for the behavior
for the first time as the result of a demonstration, and
apparently the same situation was present the second time.
Juan followed only a few days subsequent to the visit.
Neither of the two men saw any connection between the
visit and their acquisition of the behavior: Juan viewed it
mainly as resulting from God's intention to give him a sign
concerning his ministry, and Salvador related it to the fact
of his wife's conversion. It seemed to me, however, that a
learning situation was involved and so at the end of the
same year I went to visit the congregation that had sent the
group, the Reverend Frank Munsey and his Evangelical
Temple of Hammond, Indiana. The findings of this trip will
be discussed later.

3. *Trinidad.* Trinidad is a housewife, about fifty years

old, a shade better dressed than most of the other older
women of the congregation. She is heavy-set and has a
strong, intelligent face, more Spanish than Indian in its
features. Her voice is deep and confident. She comes to the
church every Sunday from a small hamlet outside the city;
the trip takes her three quarters of an hour. Of her six
children, four are converted. One of her daughters usually
accompanies her to the service.

Trinidad A. L., Mexico City, Summer 1968
    I was converted more than twenty years ago. I first
heard the Gospel in a Methodist church, but later an
hermano also spoke to me about this church and that
it received the promise of the Holy Spirit, and so I wanted
to come and know it. We studied the Gospel, the principal
epistles, the Acts, what Jesus did and the Apostles, and
how it is written that one should be baptized in the name
of Jesus Christ so one's sins will be forgiven and he will
receive the gift of the Holy Spirit. All of this we studied,
and I liked it very much.
    Then the *hermanos* said, "Let's pray now to the Lord,
so that God may give the manifestation of the Holy Spirit."
And although at that time I had not heard about these
things, nor did I know anything about them, I also received
the promise of the Holy Spirit [glossolalia]. We were
six *hermanas* altogether. [Here her ordinarily strong and
deep voice changes, breaking and continuing very low.]
It was very beautiful, *Hermana*, very beautiful, because one
has a spiritual contact, and while still being on this earth
one feels a joy, and during these moments you don't know
what to do, you feel a spiritual delight, a spiritual presence
of the Lord, and this is what makes you shout, full of
emotion, this divine power that manifests itself in you.
Some people that were visiting us at the time wanted to
run out of the church because they thought that something
had happened to us, but no—it was only the glorious
manifestation that the Lord gives to his children.
    Afterward one feels joyful, wanting to glorify the Lord.
This manifestation never leaves you. Do you know in
what way it will only leave you? If you offend God.
If you commit transgressions, if you commit something

that is not proper. Then, that is it. Many *hermanos* have
told me that they went and did wrong. And then
they no longer received this benediction of the Lord. The
Lord leaves. As for me, I kneel to pray, I feel contact,
and I speak in tongues. I may be washing the dishes,
and the Lord may be telling me to speak in tongues,
whether I am alone or with others. It may happen to me
on the market, or walking down a road, wherever it may be.
It doesn't matter, for it is the same benediction that the
Lord also gives me here in the church.

The new information emerging from this conversion
story concerns the seemingly erratic manner in which glossolalia behavior overtakes the practitioner: in just about
every ordinary life situation Trinidad may feel the urge to
speak in tongues. The borderline between the conscious
state and dissociation appears so indistinct, so obliterated,
that crossing it becomes an adventitious occurrence. In the
case of Salvador, we saw a similar spontaneous trance
event, but there it was probably called forth by the context
of the conversion story. What triggering mechanism, if any,
is present with Trinidad, we do not know, but whatever it
is, she is obviously not aware of it.

4. *Maria-Luisa.* Maria-Luisa is sixty-eight years old, and
she takes in washing for a living. She is unmarried (having
lived briefly in consensual union, a pattern very frequently
encountered in Latin America), her only daughter died a
few years ago, and now "only God and I are in my house."
She is dark, very slender, and has white hair that she wears
in a braid. Her clothes are worn and faded but always clean,
usually a long gathered skirt and a long-sleeved blouse, a
white, crocheted mantilla. She wears glasses with very thick
lenses, which emphasize the delicateness of her features.
Like nearly everyone in the congregation (at one count,
forty-two of the forty-eight adults present), she was not
born in the capital.

Maria-Luisa T. A., Mexico City, Summer 1968
I was converted about ten years ago. Until then I
didn't know that there was any other religion but the

Catholic one. One day I heard a song. It was the one that
begins, "*En la cruz, en la cruz. . . .*" I heard it while going
by bus to Cuernavaca, up there by Tacubaya, where there
are many churches. Well, I heard this song, and it impressed
me a great deal. I went searching to find out who was
singing that song, but I could not find where the singers
were. However, I knew that I was a Catholic, and that all
the other people were Catholics, and we were not happy.
And I also thought, well, those images of the saints in the
churches, they don't move, they don't even look nice, and
yet it is said that they perform miracles. I just could not
believe that. I felt that there must be something else,
something better, but I did not know what. However, with
this interest, I kept on searching. I encountered many
people who told me that Catholicism was the true religion
of Christ. But although it was their religion, they didn't
try to understand it. I kept thinking: if only I could meet
someone who would be able to talk to me and tell me of
something better. And I would talk to people in the buses,
on the roads, things like that.

Finally I met a woman, and she said, "Come to my
house, and I will take you to some Baptists, and perhaps
you will like that." And I asked her, "Do you think that
theirs is the real, the true religion?" And she said, "Well,
the real religion is in the Bible, which all of the churches
have, but not all churches do what God tells them to do.
In other words, there are churches that are disobedient
to God." She wanted to give me a Bible, but I didn't
know how to read.

Finally I met another woman, and she took me to this
church, here in Mexico City, which was the real one. This
was on the first day of the year, which is in January.
Only I still didn't know how to read. But I wanted to enter
into the creed completely, and I was angry and I cried,
and feeling in this way, and with all that enthusiasm of mine,
I learned to read. I waited just one month, and I became
baptized. And I felt a beautiful benediction, and without
any shame or embarrassment, I went to the altar railing,
and I went down on my knees, and there I was saying,
"*Gloria Christi, Gloria Christi,*" and the blessing I felt—

oh!—but how beautiful I felt! And every day after that, no matter who was present at the church, I always went to the altar, and I always gave testimony, because after all, now I also had heard many sermons, and I was not so ignorant any more.

Then finally, on the fifteenth day of August, I was baptized by the Holy Spirit. This feels wonderful. It is very difficult for me to explain, but one feels delight, and one doesn't care that people are looking on, that they see the foolish things one does, one shouts, one despairs, cries, well, anyway, it is a very, very strong emotion, you feel as if your veins would burst open; well, anyway, it is a very beautiful thing.

After that, I kept forcing myself to experience that again. The other people said that I had already received the baptism of the Holy Spirit, but still, it continued giving me something like a sadness, or a delight, I don't know what. Again and again, I would arrive here at the altar railing and would shout here [her voice falters at this spot and she breaks into tears], and the *hermanas* would say afterward, what a beautiful service it had been. And I would say, "*Pues*, I don't really know, it is always the same for me, it is always branches off the same tree."

This went on for a year. And during this whole year, food just didn't agree with me. I ate, but everything I ate, I vomited out again. At night, always only at night, I kept having a very high temperature. It was a terrible fever, and I felt that God had put me into a sort of prison and was testing me. Every night, this temperature came, and the next day, this praying in tongues came to me again. My daughter would bring me food, but I kept telling her that I was not hungry, and I didn't eat, I continued praying, and I cried, and I suffered a great deal. I don't remember much about that time. The pastor said to me, "What's the matter with you? You are so thin." And I said, "*Pues*, I don't eat, I am not hungry." And the pastor said, "What good is salvation to you if you don't eat?" I became very, very thin. After all, flesh will be flesh, *¿verdad?*

Finally, my daughter took me to a doctor, and he said that I had a very severe anemia, and he cured me.

Since then, I have been better. I am very happy with God.
There is no one like God. In the world, one suffers much.
But I am happy.

We can analyze this extraordinary reaction to the acquisition of glossolalia behavior on various levels. Maria-
Luisa's condition is characterized by inappetence, vomiting
of the food she does ingest, and fever at night. With respect
to behavior, there is a general lowering of inhibition; she
shouts, cries, and cannot control her comportment. She
perceives of herself as being enclosed in a prison; the experience is so intense that her veins seem to burst open, and
due to this very intensity, she is unable to decide whether
to label what she undergoes as positive or negative. Is it
wonderful or sad? Delightful and beautiful, or bringing
suffering and despair? There is also doubt as to the capability for volition: she has no control over the glossolalia,
it comes again and again, every day during that first year,
and yet she reports that she forces herself to experience it
over and over. And finally, she is aware that she does not
have much memory of the details of what happened during
that time span. The liberation, if we want to call it that, the
recovery, comes with the treatment for anemia, i.e., there is
some manipulation and medication involved. At the time
of the observation, she is cheerful and relaxed. I never hear
any recordable loud glossolalia from her, and I see no striking movements, only an occasional flow of tears.

5. *Lorenzo.* The minister of the Utzpak congregation in
1969 and 1970 is a salesman by profession. Born in 1944,
he is light complexioned, rather stout, with an affable
manner, but in church he is a severe taskmaster. He is a
gifted orator, lacing his sermons with Maya phrases (although he is a native Spanish speaker) and serving up a
heady mixture of sophistication and fire and brimstone.
He was born and raised in Campeche, the second largest
city of the Yucatecan Peninsula and capital of the state by
the same name. His wife, a native Maya speaker, comes
from Campeche also. They have two small sons.

Lorenzo, pastor, Utzpak, Yucatán, Summer 1969

I left home when I was fourteen years old. I was
disobedient, very rebellious, and would have none of the
discipline of my home. I was working in Campeche, doing
this and that, and it was there that I happened to hear a boy
singing the hymn that you now also know quite well,
which begins, "*Más allá del sol, más allá del sol, tengo
un hogar, bello hogar, más allá del sol.* . . . " The boy's name
was Canšók, and I very much wanted his friendship, and
I wanted him to teach me that hymn. We did become
friends, and he was the first one to tell me about the Gospel.
It made a tremendous impression on me. When I first
realized that everything in the Bible was God's word
and true, I spent days crying over my own fate and how
I was going to perdition. After a while, though, we separated,
and I forgot about God. I started on a bad life, with smoking
and drinking, and drugs, and women, well, just everything
that you can imagine. When I met Canšók again, about
a year and a half later, we were so far apart, we couldn't
even greet each other any more. I couldn't face him. I was
married, and then I met Gilberto, a minister of this church.
He was a salesman for the same house for which I was
collecting agent. By this time I was heartily sick of myself;
I was drinking a bottle of *aguardiente* every day; I had an
incurable illness [sinusitis], for which I had already
been operated on twice; well, I was a mess. Gilberto
started talking to me of the Gospel and finally I asked him
how I could change my life. "Kneel down there at the altar
and humble yourself." "There is no altar here," I said.
"There is an altar anywhere where a man kneels down and
confesses his sins to God." Well, I figured I would try it,
and I would make God a proposition. I said, "All right,
Lord, help me to stop drinking and smoking, and I'll
serve you." And I humbled myself, and confessed my sins
to the Lord, and asked for his forgiveness, and the Lord
worked his miracle on me. It wasn't that I told myself
that I would not smoke or drink any more; I did not want
to any more. I would go to taverns to collect and there
would be beer, and *aguardiente*, and it just didn't represent
any temptation for me any more. And the Lord made me
healthy. Things went well for a while, but after a time,

a person may become weak. You become, we might say,
cold. One day, the family of my wife gave a fiesta. They
are rich, you see. My father was very rich, too, from cattle
trading, then started gambling away his money. He was
always accompanied by two *pistoleros* [body guards].
He lived at night and slept in the daytime, until he died
of an embolism. One of my brothers let me have a house
when I was married, but when I became converted they
threw me out in the street. I had intended to stay away,
but I got so weak that I went just to smell the tobacco.
I thought, I wouldn't smoke, just smell it again. The men
of the family started taunting me, saying why wouldn't
I stay and have a real binge, something like lasting for
a week, for this is how they do things. I said, all right,
I'll do it. Then I don't know how or why, but Gilberto
came to the door, and I went to open it, and we started
talking, and instead of a week's binge, we went to pray.
However, I still was not firm enough. Man is weak.
Also, I was unhappy because my wife refused to be
converted. That is a great burden to bear. There came
a friend, and he led me into some illegal activity. In the
course of it, I lost everything, my equipment, my truck,
well, everything I owned, and I was left with a pile of debts.
But with God's help, I soon accumulated the several
thousand pesos that I owed. God is truly powerful.
I delivered myself up to the Lord to be his slave for all
my life, and he has given me his mercy. Finally also my
wife became converted.

After I was baptized, I prayed for the Holy Spirit long
and hard but did not receive it. There was one time when
I cried and cried, and I was bathed in perspiration, and
I saw a light, but I did not receive the gift of tongues:
it was my companion who did. But the next time it was also
given to me. It is a lovely experience the first time, something
you can hardly describe; there was a pressure on my chest,
I felt as if I were being lifted up bodily, and my tongue
felt swollen. At first it is not possible to control the
manifestation in any way, and it is such a pleasure.
Well, the flesh is weak, and man is what he is; you want
to have it all the time. But prayer is also to serve to edify
others, and when you speak in tongues, no one present

can understand you. So after a while I learned to contain myself to a certain extent and also use ordinary language prayer. The gift of tongues is a true benediction of the Lord.

This is an account of a series of relapses, of a struggle against losing hold on what is seen as salvation, as the new life. We are told of two catastrophic episodes of this nature, one after separating from Cansók, the other after considerable contact with the minister Gilberto. There are hints of additional, perhaps less dangerous, ones. We are led to believe that with the acquisition of glossolalia behavior—which he has honed into a surpreme professional tool and of which he loses control only under exceptional circumstances, as we shall see—the new Adam is truly born, never to fall again. I would venture to suggest that the mazeway resynthesis, as Anthony F. C. Wallace calls it (1961:152), this making over the personality under the effect of acquiring the capability of entering into an altered state of consciousness (I am stating it more generally; Wallace speaks of a hallucinatory trance) is once more in the process of being undone. In 1970, upon revisiting the Utzpak congregation, I perceived a change in the general tenor of his sermons. The good humor and joviality of the previous year had almost disappeared. Instead, there were somber tones, and threats of eternal damnation abounded. He seemed continually on a quixotic errand against *las suciedades del mundo*, the filth of the world. Everything was *suciedad*—scientific theories, diversions, sex problems, even words he was not familiar with such as *eschatology*, which he accorded this translation in a Bible-school session. At the same time there were mounting allegations in the congregation that he was misspending the church's money. He began making frequent trips to Campeche and in the middle of July requested to be transferred there.

What I propose is that he perceived a weakening, an attenuation of the impact of the trance experience, and that possibly his increasing fanaticism was an expression of his attendant anxiety. Perhaps the revitalization movement that he helped trigger late in July 1970 will help stave off another relapse, but the question is for how long.[2]

6. *Nohoč Felipe* (*Felipe, Senior*). Nohoč Felipe is a Maya Indian, a *milpa* (cornfield) farmer, sixty-three years old, lean and muscular, unpretentious, always ready to laugh. He plays the mouth organ, the guitar, and the *marimbol* and loves to sing. He learned to read only a few years ago so that he could study the Bible, which he does whenever he can find the time. He and his wife Eusebia had nine children, eight of them living, all adults; one of his sons is an ordained pastor of the Apostolic church, another son and a daughter have also been baptized, while two daughters are active sympathizers.

Before passing on to his narration, it might be of interest to give here a section of his wife's conversion story, also recorded in 1969.

Eusebia, Utzpak, Yucatán, Summer 1969

I have a friend called Doña Valuch. She is the wife of *Hermano* Tacho. About ten years ago she invited me to attend some services the *hermanos* were holding in her house. I had been a Catholic before, but there is no certainty with the Catholics. Catholics don't believe in God, they believe in the statues of saints, that they can do miracles. But in Mérida, I have seen how they make these statues. They make them from *saskáb* [white earth], and then they paint them. After that, the *cura* blesses them, and already they can do miracles. Once there was no rain, and Nohoč Felipe was about to lose his harvest. So I went to Tizimin, to pray to the famous *Tres Reyes* [Three Kings] there. I bought a big candle for three pesos, and every morning for a week I went there, carrying the big candle, and prayed three Salvos, [popular for "Salve," prayer in honor of the Virgin Mary], as I had promised, and listened to the mass. Then I went home, but a few days later I came back for a second week. This is how they tell you to do it: you have to come for three weeks. But when I got home

---

[2] For the history and an analysis of the tranced-based upheaval that occurred in Utzpak after the completion of this manuscript see Goodman 1971c.

the second time, Nohoč Felipe's harvest was already lost
for the sun, and so I never went back for a third week,
for it was clear that those Kings could perform no miracles.

At first, I went alone to the services in Doña Valuch's
house, and took only Nina along [her youngest daughter,
nine years old at the time]. Nohoč Felipe would say,
"Kó²oš, let's go to the movies." But I would answer,
"You go alone, you just give me the money for my ticket."
And with that I would go to the service, and contribute
it in the offering.

One evening, it was very dark, so Nohoč Felipe took
me to Doña Valuch's house with his flashlight. I said,
"Why don't you come in?" So he did, and from then on
he did not go to the *cine* any more, but only to the services.
He would still smoke, and if I objected he would go out
to the *solar* [garden around the house] to do it. I said,
"From me you can hide, but from Jesus you cannot."
So he stopped, and that cured his asthma. Eventually, he
also stopped drinking.

Now here is Felipe, Utzpak, Yucatán, Summer 1969

The *hermanos* were holding some services in the house
of *Hermano* Tacho and, going for a walk, I would stop
on the corner to hear what they were doing. I kept doing
this for a long time.

So, while Nohoč Felipe was supposedly at the movies he
was actually already trying to find out something about
these services. He is not really spying on his wife's activities
but rather carefully weighing the value of the new attraction
before committing himself by open attendance. Ermela,
another *hermana*, tells of the similar behavior of her husband:

I used to be a Catholic, but never understood anything
of the services. I heard about the *hermanos*, and Gilberto
spoke to me about the Gospel and invited us to come
to Mérida to attend the services. I went alone with my
mother-in-law, Pola, and we took the little ones. Valentin
would say, "Where are you women going, don't you have
anything to do?" But we continued going anyway.

Valentin enjoyed the things of the world, he drank,
he smoked, he was *muy parrandista*—out for fun. Finally
he couldn't stand it any longer, he was curious to see what
the services were like, and he accompanied us. He would
not show himself openly, just stay in the dark, in the back,
his cigarettes in his pocket. He kept coming, and gradually
realized that this religion was the right thing. He stopped
smoking, and left the other things of the world behind.

We will encounter the same pattern once more in Emilio's
story. This is quite a different approach than the emotional
appeal to which the people respond in the big city, epito-
mized by Maria-Luisa's "Once on the way to Tacubaya I
heard a song . . . ," or the bargaining with God of such men
as Juan, Salvador, or Lorenzo.

Amusingly, and by the way, Nohoč Felipe does not mention his wife inviting him:

Finally they asked me, "Are you always just going to stand
on the corner listening?" So I started going to the services,
and I also went to the services in the house of Don Carrillo.
And everything they said became fixed in my mind.
Finally, I decided to become converted. I say to myself,
"What I have done, I have done. It is already behind me.
Maybe Christ will accept me. I am going to follow him,
and I'll see where that will take me. I'll follow him,
I don't know where to." Then the *hermanos* said, "You
will have to get legally married. Whoever is not married
will not be accepted by Christ." When I hear this,
I immediately say, "*Pues*, let's go to it." And the *hermanos*
came, and they held a wedding service, and we killed turkeys
for *tacos*, and we served everybody Pepsi Cola. Before
I was converted, things were quite different. We served
Habanero [a hard liquor], and beer on the day *de mi Santo*
[name day], and what expenses we had! And these drunkards
that we would invite, we would serve them one day, and
then they'd come back the following day to be served
again. With the *hermanos*, it is not like that. What you
spend, you spend, and that's it.
     I was baptized about three years ago. They baptized
us together, five of us, there at Santa Clara, where we are

going tomorrow. The spot where they hold the baptism
is about a league away from Santa Clara, following
the highway. It is beautiful, there at the seashore; there
is a beach, you can go, and go, and go, and there are many
coconut trees. When the baptism is over, the people come
to eat, and they take their *čan almuerzo* [little lunch] under
the trees, lots of people, lots of souls, very nice.

Before I was converted, I belonged to the Catholic
church. I was very devout, I took boxes of votive candles
to the church. The *cura* [priest] would say, "Come, my
little sons, I will free you of your sins. Come on such and
such a day, at seven or at six, early in the morning."
So he would promise to free us of our sins, and he a bigger
sinner than we were! [He laughs.] This showed me that
of these *curas* none gave any certainty. They suck
everything from their thumb. Another thing I didn't like
was the matter of the images that they say we should
adore. They are not as holy as they maintain. The Holy One
is sitting up there on his celestial throne, nobody knows
him, nobody can reach up to him. They make them of
stone, of cardboard, of gypsum, in all sorts of forms,
but they have no intestines whatever, they have no blood
at all, they are not the work of Christ. We are the ones
that are his work, for no matter where we get scratched,
no matter with what, we bleed, even from our fingers.

After the baptism, my life certainly changed. Before,
I would leave home with twenty-five pesos or twenty, and
when I would come back, I would not even have five
centavos left. Now when I go out, I leave with five pesos,
and I come back with 4.50 or 3.50. Also, I am happy,
for we always go singing happy songs, and there I am in
the church, very gay, I grab my guitar, and it all sounds
so full of joy.

I have even been baptized already by the Holy Spirit.
I have spoken in other tongues, not in Spanish, and every
word seems to come out upside down, and you ask yourself,
what might that be? For they are words that you don't
understand, and yet they keep coming. And when the
Holy Spirit comes, it feels as if my head were swelling up,
but real big, and then it becomes small once more, I
don't know how, and this feeling reaches down into the

legs, and the middle of the back. It grabs you, and you feel the Lord's power, there is nothing like it, and nothing will stop it. So this is all the matter that I have done.

In addition to the revealing description of the altered state of consciousness, or rather of the modified perceptions during this state, Nohoč Felipe's account is significant in showing what social changes are brought about in joining the congregation: new friends are acquired, the economic posture is altered, a different type of community life is entered. He experiences glossolalia and later engages in the behavior not for its own sake, not for the joy or the release it might possibly bring, but because it is the fulfilling of an obligation incurred by joining the group. Another *hermano* ticks these obligations off on his fingers: "I got married, I was baptized by water, today also by the Holy Spirit, all that remains now is that I also start tithing." This could have been said by Nohoč Felipe, too.

7. *Emilio.* Emilio is also a Maya peasant, twenty-four years old at the time of this narration. He and his wife have two children. He is very gentle, retiring, and has a mouthing, slow manner of speaking. When talking with anyone, he projects the impression of continually defending himself against some unspoken reproach. He rarely smiles. In 1969, when I started recording his glossolalia, he had "learned" (see chap.'s. 3–5) the behavior only six months previously. His utterances at that time were quite long, often extending over ten minutes or more, with hardly any kinetic manifestation accompanying them. We shall see later how all this changed by the summer of 1970.

Emilio, Utzpak, Yucatán, Summer 1969
I went to live with a girl when I was fourteen years old. I could not marry her legally because for that you have to be fifteen. She was sixteen at the time. We had a son, but later I left her and married again when I was nineteen, in the Catholic church, to please my mother. My mother also made me attend masses, but I didn't go very often. I used to drink all the time, and then I slept in the street

until the next morning, in front of the *cantina* or someplace
like that. Or I would play cards all night and lose all
my earnings. Sometimes I would go to the services of the
Presbyterians but didn't think much of them. They go
to movies, or dances, so obviously their dogma cannot
be the truth. I kept on feeling this anxiety, this fear
[*ese temor*].

One day, *Hermano* Nicolas and *Hermano* Valentin went
to pray for Don Vicente, who since then is dead. I stood
on the street corner and listened to how they prayed.
When *Hermano* Nicolas came out of the house, he saw me
standing there and began talking to me. He talked with
me many more times, and he invited me to the services.
So I went. I liked what he said in his sermons, that we
should not fight, that if we had a second woman we
should leave her. Before we were baptized, another pastor
also came to teach us, and then we were baptized with
water, and from then on I felt a great fear if I thought
about going to a dance, or about playing pool, and I never
did it again. A month later I was also baptized by the
Holy Spirit. Now I am afraid no longer.

We might recall that Juan also hinted at a relief from
anxiety through the experience of glossolalia. "Afterward,
all my problems were forgotten." Emilio, however, explicitly
spells this out; in fact, it seems the very center of his experience. Even before contact with the *Apostolicos*, he is
beset by *temor*, dread, fear, what the German calls *Angst*.
In addition to the Presbyterians, I was told by my informants, he also sought out the other Protestant denominations, Latter-Day Saints and Baptists. After the baptism
with water in the Apostolic church, this apparently diffuse
anxiety becomes focused on sin: *cine, baile, tomar, fumar*
is the ever-repeated formula in the congregation—picture
shows, dances, drinking, smoking. Resolution of it does
not come until a month later with the experience of speaking
in tongues. This is a very important key to understanding
Emilio's comportment a year later.

8. *Chela*. Chela, a Maya peasant woman, was married
at fourteen. Her husband is a *vaquero* and in charge of some

of the vast herds of cattle of a *ranchero* living in Utzpak.
As such, his income is slightly better than average, but the
expenses of Pedrito's illness have vastly overextended the
family's resources. Pedrito is Chela's eighth child (she was
expecting her ninth in August 1970), and he has polio. The
Mexican government distributes polio vaccine free of charge
to all, but Pedrito's family lived on a ranch when he was
born and his parents neglected to take him to the clinic in
Utzpak. Besides, he caught the disease when he was only a
few months old.

Chela, Utzpak, Yucatán, Summer 1969
    Once, when I was a very small girl, I saw a saint.
People said that he performed miracles and that he was
so much alive that he even moved his feet. He was standing
there, practically buried in flowers. So I went up to him
and through the flowers put my hands on his feet. I found
them cold and rigid: they were made of gypsum. From
then on, I didn't listen any more to what people said
about the saints.
    As I grew older, I used to go to the Catholic services,
but I did not worry too much about sinning. You could
always go and confess, and then things were right again.
And I continued going to movies and dances.
    When my father, Don Carrillo, became acquainted with
the Gospel and started attending the services that *Hermano*
Oscar Gill [a Mexican evangelist] conducted, he also
told us children about it. He used to be a *torero*, but at
that time he decided to give up the things of the world.
Now, however, he once more has the Demon in his heart.
He keeps talking about religion, but he curses people,
and he doesn't really believe in anything. I was interested
in what he said about the Gospel, for I never did understand
anything the *cura* said during the mass, because it was
all in Latin. I had even gone to some of *Hermano* Gruber's
services [an American Baptist missionary who occasionally
comes to Utzpak].
    When Pedrito became sick with polio, when he was
only a few months old, I had him baptized in the Catholic
church, for people say that such a baptism will cure a child.
But that isn't true, for it didn't cure Pedrito. The *cura*

says that when he blesses the water it becomes sacred, but
he doesn't really change the water, it doesn't cure. The *cura*
acts as if he were a *yerbero* [a man who makes decoctions
from herbs for medicinal use], but of course, he isn't one.

Occasionally, Pastor Felipe would come by and would
talk to the children, but I didn't want to hear what he said
and would close my door when I saw him coming. But
little Pedrito was getting worse, so one day I finally
decided to ask *Hermano* Felipe to pray over him. He had
his guitar with him, and he told me that I would have to
kneel down and cover my head and pray with him.
After the prayer, he sang a beautiful hymn. This touched
my heart. I started praying on my own, and also began
going to the services in the church.

Even in church, however, I didn't feel happy. I always
worried so much about Pedrito. I was afraid that he might
catch cold on the way to church, or in it, or that he might
get sicker if I took him, so many times I didn't go to the
service. Finally, I received the Holy Spirit. The night before
that happened, I dreamt that I should fast, and then the
Holy Spirit would baptize me, and that is how it was.
Now I don't worry about him getting sicker any more.
I take him to church whenever there is a service, and
I don't cover him so tightly either any more. He has not
got sicker, and even his fever is less.

On 4 August, I was baptized with water in the seaport
of Santa Clara. For ten days before that baptism Pedrito
would not eat, and he had a fever. I was afraid to go to be
baptized, but then I did it anyway. After our baptism we
carried Pedrito into the water of the ocean, and we prayed
over him, the *hermanos* and I. In the water he seemed
to move his legs a little, and afterward he started eating
again and he has no fever any more. My husband was
also baptized on the same day. God has granted me
everything I asked for. Later, when we walked from the
seashore to the truck to go home, I heard many hymns
being sung very loudly, but they were not sung by the
hermanos. They were being sung in a very great temple.

What is important in this account, I think, is the evidence
about hallucination that it offers. Also a hyperarousal
phenomenon, it is apparently not produced by such external

stimuli as those involved in "driving," a strategy for inducing trance (to be discussed in the next chapter). Visual observation of her behavior and her vocalization had shown Chela to be in trance during the prayer for Pedrito alluded to above, and she may have continued in residual arousal, a trance phase we shall discuss in the chapter on waking. This, coming on top of the emotional upheaval of the baptism, may have pushed her into the peak experience of an auditory hallucination despite the relaxation offered by the brief picnic that followed the baptismal ceremony. (According to her description, the incident took place on her walk from the seashore to the truck. The walk thus led across some bare stretches of sand, then along a path with palm trees lining it on one side, and then to a small group of huts. No one was singing either on the path or in any of the homes, and there was no radio audible.)

9. *Gregoria.* Gregoria is a native Maya speaker who came to the city of Mérida as an adult. She is a widow and the mother of the pastors Gilberto and Nicolas. She also has a daughter, who is tolerant of her religious activities but uninterested, and a third son, who is not converted and whom no one ever mentions in her house. For a woman in her sixties she has a strong and slender body, but her face is deeply lined, her hair gray, and she has few teeth left. In glossolalia, she usually rocks up and down, and at the high points she stretches out her arms and her hands flutter very rapidly back and forth as in a grotesquely speeded-up motion of hailing someone. She also sings in trance. Her home is the center of much of the community activity of the Mérida congregation, and she always has some vacant hooks where an *hermano* passing through the city can hang his hammock.

Gregoria, Mérida, Yucatán, Summer 1969
  One night God revealed himself to me, and I saw this great light in the shape of a hand, and it was very brilliant. And with this light I heard a voice saying, "Your son Gilberto will be a prophet, and he will receive the gift of the Holy Spirit when he is twenty-one years old."

Then the voice also said, "You will become sick, but you
will not die. You will recover." I continued seeing that
light, and it sent out many rays. And God said, "You have
a sister, and she has two daughters. These two girls will
be lost."

I woke up crying and shaking. But then I heard the
voice again, saying, "Your grandson will become a prophet
when he is nineteen years old. You have the pictures of
saints in your house. Those don't serve you, they are
disturbing you: get rid of them." After that God gave me
a sign, and I saw white angels, and [with increasing
enthusiasm] I saw white horses going by, and his white
flag going by, very, very white.

After that, I woke up completely transformed. I thought
about what God had told me, and wondered how that
would be that my life would change.

In the morning, with such ease, I took down all the
pictures of saints I had and threw them out on the trash
pile. [For attitudes toward the Catholic church in this sect
see Goodman 1971c.]

Time passed by rapidly; during the next three or four
days I kept speaking about God, and then I became ill.
My entire body was shaking and trembling, and I could
walk only along the walls and holding on to them, and I
could not straighten up. I was taken to a hospital, but I
knew that God was walking beside me. He even gave me
another vision, I saw an enormous book, which was the
Holy Bible, attached to the door of the hospital. And he
gave me to say to my son Gilberto that he would do the
work of God, and would perform thousands of miracles.

After the examination in the hospital, I went home and
started cleaning up the house and sweeping. It was about
six in the evening, and suddenly I knew nothing and
lost consciousness.

Three days later I woke up; there was a doctor attending
me, and there were my brothers, my younger sister,
my daughter, my sons. My son Gilberto told me that he
had been listening to the Gospel, and that he wanted
to be baptized. This surprised me a great deal, for he had
been a very bad boy. This was just after his twenty-first
birthday.

Some days later, my son Gilberto sent *Hermano* Oscar
Gill to my house. He said that was the *hermano* that had
converted him. He was to pray for me. I said, "Why do
you want to do that? There is no help for me. God wants
to take me away." But Gilberto said, "Let him try to do
something for you." And the *hermano* prayed for me, and
spoke to me about how great were the things of God. But
you see, I was already converted. Anyway, this was on a
Thursday. On Friday, my trembling was already better,
and I began going to the services in the church. I felt even
better, and slowly I did not feel any of the trembling any
more. My husband asked me, "What is going on? What
are they doing for you?" And I said, "Nothing but praying.
You should also go to the church, and leave your vices
behind, and you would be a different man." But he would
not do it.

The beginning of January, I started going to church,
and at the beginning of February I received the Holy Spirit.
I had prayed for it, and then I felt the heat, the heat of the
Lord, it reached up to my neck, and I saw the great light,
it was like one of those very large lamps, and I began to
weep. Then I began to speak in tongues, and I began to pray
and pray. And this is how my conversion was.

But you see, when I received the Gospel, I had already
been converted. I was converted directly by God, by the
power, because he showed me that light, and speaking
to me, he was already converting me. And when I woke
up after that, I already began speaking of God, and he told
me what to do, and I did it. And all the things he told me
about came true. My son Gilberto was converted, and soon
after that my sister came to see me. She said, "They say
that you heard a voice." I said, "That's right, I did,
and the voice said that you should watch out, because
your two daughters will be lost." And she said, very
angrily, "What are you, anyway? Are you a Spiritist that
you talk that way, or are you doing witchcraft?" And I
answered, "Witchcraft? Witchcraft, nothing. It was while
I was asleep, it was God's voice that told me that."

She began to cry, and I said, "Don't cry, I am getting
much better, and I firmly believe that one day I'll be
completely well." And she said, "I am not crying about you,

I am crying because my daughters are already lost."
And that was true, for one of them, only thirteen years old,
was five months pregnant, and the older one, seven months.
So what God told me in my dream, it all came true.

And so, *Hermana*, I shall serve him all the days of my
life.

Gregoria, we should note here, is the only one of the
ten informants quoted (and also the only one of all the
twenty-nine informants consulted) who views her initial
hallucinatory experience as the true locus of her conversion.
Her account strikingly parallels the classical shamanistic
pattern: vision, which incorporates the call, extended loss
of consciousness, illness, recovery, and service (see, e.g.,
Lommel's presentation, 1965).

10. *Nicolas.* The youngest of Gregoria's three sons,
Nicolas is unmarried; he was born and raised in Mérida. He
is a wrought-iron worker by trade but now works mostly as
a salesman. A slender, dark man with a strident voice, he is
a very effective preacher, his natural gift for oratory aug-
mented by several years' training at various Bible institutes.
Two visits to a congregation in California have added to
his sophistication without diminishing his evangelizing fervor.

Nicolas, Mérida, Yucatán, Summer 1969
I used to live like everyone else, sinning. Especially,
I used to like to go to dances. My brother Gilberto used
to tell me about the Gospel, but I wasn't really interested.
Then my father died, and there was a special service.
I went, not to hear the Gospel, but only out of courtesy
to my mother and my brother. I liked the singing, but the
rest of the service didn't really impress me. However,
I did go next Sunday again, more out of boredom than
interest. The following week goes by, I go again, and
another, and already I like the service better. I don't
particularly pray for the Holy Spirit. I saw my mother
receive its baptism [he imitates the very typical fluttering
movement of her hands], and it frightened me. There is an
altar call, and just so that I would not feel out of place,
I go up to the altar with the others. All of a sudden I feel

myself to be the greatest sinner in all the world. I start
praying in a very loud voice, asking for forgiveness, and
suddenly I become aware that I am standing there, before
the altar, all alone, and I am puzzled. Another week goes
by and a friend comes and says, "Let's go dancing."
So I take my bath, and I say, "*Pues*—let's go." For a while
we stand there across from the dance hall, looking. Finally
my friend says, "Why don't we go in?" So we cross the
street to go in, when all of a sudden I hear a voice.
Very clearly it says, "*No entras aquí, no es tu lugar*"—
"don't enter here, you don't belong here." This was the
turning point for me. From then on, I started going to
services regularly. I was baptized, and a few weeks later
I also received the gift of tongues. So you see, I think that
I really received the baptism of the Holy Spirit at that time
when I understood that I was a sinner. It must be possible,
therefore, to be baptized by the Holy Spirit even without
speaking in tongues. But for the church, for the
congregation, the gift of tongues is the outward sign.
This is how the congregation knows that the Holy Spirit
really baptized the person. The other kind of baptism
only God knows. After speaking in other tongues, the
person remains with joy and with the hope that God
will keep his promise of salvation.

Nicolas pinpoints the altered state of consciousness
rather than speaking in tongues as the focus of his conversion experience. In his mind, the glossolalia represents a
superimposed behavior with important functions within the
group. This experiential interpretation agrees strikingly with
the finding, to be detailed in the next two chapters, that the
trance is achieved or learned initially and is the primary
manifestation while the glossolalia is a secondary pattern
elaborated on this substratum.

If the other nine informants were as analytical as Nicolas
they would probably agree with him. The respective statements of the various conversion accounts all point to this
conclusion. In fact, beyond the impression of diversity af-
forded by these accounts, that is one of the generalizations
they all admit.

Another generalization we can arrive at is the relative ease with which especially the trance can be achieved, the generally joyous feeling that remains as an emotional after-effect, and the different ways in which the behavior seems to broaden the individual's range of experience while enhancing the depth of his emotional capacities.

3 Altered States of Consciousness

The conversion stories of the previous chapter have provided us with some details about the way in which many glossolalists feel when they engage in speaking in tongues. From their testimony and some others not quoted in Chapter 2 we know that some of them are aware of having cried; they speak of veins seemingly bursting open, the tongue being locked in place or swollen; of being lifted up; of feeling hot, of pressure on the chest, sometimes from both sides, of cheeks ballooning, or the head swelling, then shrinking again; of gentle rain coming down on neck and shoulders and penetrating the chest; of the sensation reaching down into the legs and the middle of the back; and, as Nohoč Felipe says, "The power of the Lord grabs you, and nothing will stop it."

Apart from the flow of tears, however, the outside observer sees entirely different manifestations. These are tightly closed eyes and rapid breathing, occasionally pallor and goose pimples; a twitching and flushed face; in addition to lacrimation, salivation and perspiration; inability to swallow, rigidity of limbs, trembling, spasms; and unusual kinetic behavior such as rhythmic movements, sometimes of very great rapidity. As I pointed out, the entire behavior complex changes over time, and the patterns are most extreme when the behavior is just being learned[1] or is of

[1] "There is, in many societies, more or less systematic learning of how to develop trance states and these states are then systematically induced on the one hand and, on the other, conform to a considerable extent to a culturally constituted model" (Bourguignon 1970:187).

recent origin: I have seen such perspiration in some instances that even the upper part of the man's trousers was soaked through and heavy beads of sweat appeared on the back of another's hand; salivation so intense that afterward there were hand-sized or even larger pools of clear saliva on the cement floor of the church; inability to swallow —one girl nearly choked on her own saliva as she stretched out on a chair, her neck resting on the back of it, her heels on the floor, her legs stiff. In the Mérida congregation, a man somersaulted from one end of the church to the other, and in the Cuarta Iglesia of Mexico City I filmed a boy of eighteen who from a kneeling position propelled himself upward so rapidly that when some of my students later saw the footage they thought I had speeded up the film.

This type of behavior is in distinct contrast to certain meditative conditions (see, e.g., Hoenig 1968; Kamiya 1968; R. K. Wallace 1970) in which the person, eyes usually open, remains perfectly motionless, his pulse rate and breathing slower than normal.

The conditions into which the glossolalist or the meditating person places himself are known by many different terms in the literature: ecstasy, frenzy, trance, delirium, somnambulistic or hypnotic state, and so on. The reason for the confusing proliferation of designations (although, for some writers, they do have quite specific meanings) is because, as Ludwig points out, this "relatively uncharted realm of mental activity has been neither systematically explored nor adequately conceptualized" (1968:69). In working with my material, I evolved an admittedly preliminary set of terms. Some of these terms have been used by other researchers in different contexts, and I borrowed them because of their rather perfect fit for what I was describing.

In my terms then, when a person has removed himself from awareness of the ordinary reality surrounding him he is in an *altered mental state*. The state of the glossolalist, of the meditating person, is in this sense an *altered state of consciousness* (in German *Ausnahmezustand*, an exceptional state). As a synonym, emphasizing a different aspect of the same generalization, I use *dissociation* to characterize the subject's divorcement from ordinary reality.

In speaking of meditative states, and mindful of the lower than normal activity of certain vital functions, I have used the descriptive term *hypoaroused*. In contrast, the mental state of the glossolalist, with its obvious somatic agitation, seems to me *hyperaroused*. The alternate possibility of *overaroused* seemed to me not expressive enough of the highly agitated state many glossolalists display. When the term *trance* appears in the descriptions, it is intended as shorthand for this hyperaroused state.

Another term that may need elucidation is that of *driving*. A gifted orator may drive his audience into a high state of excitement. The shouts of the crowd are intended to drive a football team to greater exertion. Witnessing the minister in Utzpak bending down to a kneeling supplicant, shouting his glossolalia at him, punctuating the rhythm with his fist, I felt that the term *driving* was best suited to describe what was happening. In the technical literature, I found later, *driving* is employed to characterize certain experimental conditions where the subject is exposed to rhythmically spaced sound and light signals, resulting in certain brain reactions (see Neher 1962, to be discussed later).

In the following discussion I am dealing principally with hyperarousal, since this is the state of the glossolalist. In doing so, I also present some material on sleep, since it seems to me to offer some convenient analogies to the mental state to be considered here. In fact, Fischer (1969a) suggests that trance, dreaming, and hallucinatory states are on the same continuum. Field data bear this out. Thus, for example, anthropologist George N. Appell (personal communication) reports that among the Rungus of Sabah, Malaysia, skilled spirit mediums sometimes will wake from a dream in a state of trance and talking with their guardian spirits.[2] Observations linking the hyperarousal of glossolalia

---

[2] These and similar statements in the anthropological literature, including the present investigation, are based not on laboratory observation but on self-reporting of ethnographic informants, and have validity in this sense.

with hallucinatory experiences and dreaming in various
ways also come from my own informants.

Consuelo, an *hermana* from the Mérida church, tells of
the following experience:

Before going to sleep one evening recently, I started
praying in tongues, lying in my hammock. It was about
nine o'clock in the evening. I was begging God to help
me understand what I am saying while speaking in tongues,
for the more I read the Bible, the more afraid of him
I become, and I want to be able to serve him better. All of
a sudden, instead of going to sleep after praying, my head
began hurting terribly, as if it was going to split in half,
and I saw a great light. I could not stop praying until
two the following morning.

In some instances, during field observation, it is possible
to tell whether we are seeing someone experiencing a dream
or a hallucination because of the way the subject behaves
at the time of the observation:

There is a hymn, then Isaía calls for testimonies.
Vicente gets up, says a few words, then he hyperventilates,
literally pumping air very rapidly, and stretching his right
arm out stiffly before him, he goes into glossolalia, his face
suddenly flushes, his eyes open, he shouts very loudly.
Anselmo joins him with the same movement, then Floriano.
Nearly everybody, especially in the men's and the juvenile
section where they could hear what Vicente was saying,
jumps up, there is a tremendous burst of prayer. Roberta
is also in glossolalia, Vicente continues with his, is still
very tense, he is shouting again without my being able
to catch whether he is now in glossolalia or whether he is
speaking in ordinary language.

When a modicum of quiet is restored, Isaía says that
Vicente just saw Christ, a very rare vision not given to all.

Under these circumstances, even without Isaía's subsequent interpretation, no one would maintain that Vicente
was dreaming.

In other instances, however, it is not at all easy to distin)
guish between visions and dreams. As Bourguignon (1971-
points out,

While we may be able to distinguish dreams from . . .
other hallucinatory processes in the laboratory, the
anthropological situation, where we must depend
on the selfreporting of the informants, is rather
different. Whether the dreams which occur during
REM sleep are distinguished or merged with other
vivid hallucinatory experiences will depend in part
on cultural dogma.

How difficult the distinction actually is, is exemplified by
this episode related by Nina of the Utzpak congregation.

Also I once saw the Devil. This was the night before
I was to be baptized. The Demon is very keen on getting
people just before they are to be baptized. That night
I could not fall asleep. All of a sudden I saw a man behind
a glass [window pane], in working clothes, barefoot,
floating above the ground. His face was that of an ordinary
person, but not of anyone I knew. I said, "Gloria a Dios,"—
Glory to God—and he answered in Maya, "Má? Diosu,
ten, ten . . . "—"not [glory] to God, but to me, to me!"
This is how I knew that it was the Devil. So I said to myself,
"In the name of God, I am going to see who that man is."
But when I opened my eyes, he was gone.

(By the way: Nina lives in a traditional Maya mud-and-
wattle house, and there is not a single windowpane.) Such
fluid borders would not be possible between other than
closely related states, which point also emerges from anthropological research.[3]
There are still other agreements between hyperarousal
dissociation and sleep. For instance, the impression might
arise that all relations with the external environment are
interrupted during trance, but this is not so, just as it is not
so in sleep. In the following examples, cautions and instruc-

[3] "In any given case we cannot be sure that the vision experienced
by the seeker may have been a sleeping dream, a waking hallucination,
or the product of other 'imaginative processes.' (The cultural) dogma
influences not only the *reporting* of dreams and other pseudo-percep-
tions, including secondary elaborations, but also, as far as we can tell,
the subjective experience of these states" (Bourguignon 1954).

tions are taken along into the dissociation, something like
"You are holding a child—don't drop him, don't squeeze
him."

Francisca took her sleeping infant with her when she
knelt down for the altar call. She shakes while in glossolalia,
but that does not wake up the baby, and the mother
never loses her hold on the child.

The *hermana* whose guests we are in Bacalar has her
sick infant in her arms. The little girl squirms and cries,
but instead of fondling and comforting her, as she did
this afternoon, all she does is hold on to her while continuing
with a very loud glossolalia utterance. Finally, the child
goes to sleep, her head resting on her mother's shoulder,
and is being shaken by the rhythmical tremors of the
dissociation.

I am observing Emilio. During the last prayer, he has
not got up to come and kneel at the altar. He stays in his
seat, for his four-year-old son has gone to sleep on his lap.
He goes into dissociation. The trance is light, he rocks
a little back and forth, never losing hold of his little son.
Once before I observed him with his child. At that time
he was already kneeling, and his son came to him. This
occurs all the time, even very tiny boys prefer to stick to
their fathers, no matter what the latter are doing, and are
never shooed away. In kneeling, Emilio embraced his son,
who was standing, and in considerable trance and
glossolalia he kept rocking back and forth, all the while
keeping enough control so that he never pressed the little
boy too tightly, who stayed with him to the end of the prayer.

[Some glossolalists, especially the pastors, evolve
techniques for calling up behavior. We will discuss this
later; here I should just like to anticipate, to make the
subsequent passage intelligible, that Nicolas is in the habit
of kneeling down while still holding his guitar. To induce
the trance, he then grabs its neck with both hands, and
exerting a great deal of pressure on it, he propels himself
into dissociation.]
Chela has asked Nicolas to present her polio-stricken
infant, Pedrito, to the congregation. [This takes the place

of a baptism, the *Apostolicos* do not believe in baptizing
infants.] He takes the child during this ceremony and
prays over him. Handling the child like he does the guitar,
pressing his legs and stretching them, he goes into
glossolalia. He does this with considerable control, however,
because the child only whimpers and there are no pressure
marks left on his small, pale limbs.

In addition, apparently, a "channel" is open through
which to receive stimuli from the outside world. Again,
however, as in sleep, this channel seems to be extremely
narrow: most of the stimuli are screened out. When my
children were infants, for example, I would wake up if they
as much as whimpered in the next room, but much louder
noises closer by would not wake me. What this channel may
be permeable to in hyperarousal dissociation will be discussed further on; here I only want to give some examples
of what is screened out.

Very soon, Floriano goes into trance and subsequent
glossolalia. Despite his very dark complexion, his flush
is quite visible. He is totally oblivious to the fact that
I have the camera and later the microphone trained on
him, the latter often very close to his face.

Isaía goes into a long glossolalia, finally fades into
an ordinary-language prayer. I have most of that on tape,
I am so close behind him that I have the microphone
practically at his mouth without his noticing me.

(In 1970, those in trance did not at all react to the heat of
my 1,000-watt movie light, whether it hit them full force
from the back, side, or front.)

At one point in her dissociation, Francisca breaks out
in profuse perspiration. At about the same time, one of
her little daughters, a three-year-old who continually tries
to get her mother's attention [who is nursing a one-
year-old], goes up to her from behind and unzips her very
tight dress in the back. Catching my glance, she then zips
the dress back up again: her mother never even flinches.

Anita is so deeply in trance that she does not notice that her mantilla has slipped off her head. [It is unthinkable for a woman to be in church without her head covered.] . . . Gradually, she loses her level of dissociation and becomes aware enough of herself to adjust her head covering. However, she still does not feel the cold metal of my microphone that she touched because I am so very close.

In many other respects, of course, the hyperarousal trance is quite unlike sleep. One such distinction is that concerning the lowering of inhibitions: " . . . one is not ashamed to do foolish things, cry, shout, and so on." In fact, this is apparently recognized as a hallmark of the onset of the trance, for Lorenzo tells his congregation, "If you feel anything supernatural, such as wanting to jump, or yell, give in to it, don't try to stop it, for it is the Holy Spirit trying to manifest itself." On occasion, this may lead to problems. Thus the same minister recalls:

In Jalisco the Holy Spirit possessed three men and three women, and they began to tear the clothes from their bodies there in front of the congregation. *Fijese*, what a situation for the pastor! He began beating them with his belt, and suddenly they knew where they were and started grabbing for their clothes, and their relatives in the church began dressing them.

This lowering of inhibition also extends to possibly overcoming psychosomatic disability during the trance state:

Peregrino is in charge of the first part of this evening service, and it is striking how he prefers, in the awake state, to use his left hand, and how awkwardly he holds his right arm, as if he were slightly paralyzed. Irma [one of my informants] tells me that he is nicknamed "*El Mocho*," the cripple, but neither she nor anybody else I ask seems to recall any accident. [Peregrino was born and raised in Utzpak.] However, twice I observe that in trance, when he also has a slight, clear salivation, he wipes it off with his right hand.

Perhaps due to altered perceptions about one's own body, culturally patterned inhibitions about the glossolalist's body space, that is, about the tolerable or desirable distance between himself and the next person, is also changed. Others often are not even perceived as being there, or are removed, as Consuelo relates: "I was floating a little above the ground, and one by one everybody else around me was being snatched away, upward, until I was all alone." Thus, during dissociation, the people tend to draw closer together, despite the fact that in the Utzpak church the minister would request that they guard their distance so that he could walk among them while laying on hands. This phenomenon is apparently also observable in at least one other condition of dissociation, that produced by alcohol. A student of mine was working on the use of space between speakers in communicative behavior, and she observed at a Navy ROTC ball, during a conversation with a commander who had had too much champagne punch, that he apparently had lost his ability to maintain the acceptable conversational distance.[4]

> Without thinking I began to back away from him
> as we talked. Then the words of Edward T. Hall
> (1969) flashed through my mind, and I stood my
> ground. Before long I could sense the Commander
> come closer and tower over me as I deliberately kept
> my feet still—but unconsciously compensated by
> leaning my back, shoulders, and head away from
> him [Karen Knapp, 1970, student paper].

Another feature of the trance that differs greatly from related manifestations before and during sleep is the varying amounts of observed kinetic behavior. Before human beings go to sleep, they "immobilize" themselves. What is done in this respect before achieving an altered state of consciousness of the type we are discussing does not generally involve immobilization and, moreover, differs considerably from

---

[4] The framework (and the mode of expression here) is that elaborated by Edward T. Hall in his book *The Hidden Dimension* (New York: Doubleday Anchor Books, 1969).

group to group. In the Hammond church, for example, both men and women engage in movement, although rather sparingly, raising the right arm or both arms during prayer. In the church in Mexico City, on the other hand, the men in front of the altar bow and straighten up while kneeling, raising both arms or extending one arm, then pulling it back again in a gesture often seen in Mexican orators, while the women remain kneeling practically motionless, never raising their arms. In Utzpak, neither the men nor the women move much while praying for the manifestation. These patterns are culturally structured. Thus, in the Hammond church, we find a reflection of the equality between men and women aimed at in our own society. In Mexico City, there is a considerable role distinction between men and women, the male is expected to be aggressive, mobile, the female retiring, self-effacing. In Yucatán, a great deal of decorum, expressed in very limited motion patterns, must be observed by both men and women in public.

These differences have important repercussions for achieving trance, especially for the first time. Interviews with the Hammond congregation show that both men and women go into dissociation—evidenced by the glossolalia—about equally. In the Cuarta Iglesia, on the other hand, a statistical survey of the members reveals that nearly all the women, but relatively few men, do so. The majority of the men did not experience it even once. The greatest ease in achieving the state is evidenced by the Yucatecan congregation. Fischer believes that lowering the motor component of the behavior and thus increasing the sensory input is conducive to the onset of the trance. He speaks of this phenomenon, which he terms the "high sensory to motor ratio" (1969a), as a precondition in daydreaming and also in hallucination. My observational data certainly seem to bear him out. What this means, interestingly enough, is that, although it is not practiced in many groups, to behave in the same manner as one does in preparing to go to sleep is actually helpful in achieving hyperarousal dissociation.

Viewed in this way, immobilization can be counted

among the induction strategies, to be discussed below. What a part expectation plays (which in turn is structured by the culture of the group) seems very evident even here. A person, albeit in a kneeling or standing position could conceivably go into a meditative, hypoaroused state or drop off to sleep, if this is what he expects to happen.[5]

How shifting the demarcations are, and how physiological and psychological factors blend with each other in a near-inextricable pattern, is borne out by an experience of my principal informant. Eusebia, a Maya peasant woman, fifty-nine years old at this time, had been baptized with her husband (see conversion story No. 6), and yet she seemed to have great difficulty in achieving glossolalia. "I cannot fast like the *hermanos* do," she would say, "and kneel for hours." She took comfort from the thought that, as Lorenzo told her, some people received the Holy Spirit in their hammocks just before they die. "Maybe that will happen to me too." She would attend every service given in the church, or in a private home, but would catnap with the greatest of ease, especially during the sermons. "At home I have trouble going to sleep," she would joke, "but in church I can do it right away." I was quite surprised, therefore, when her name appeared on a list of those who had been baptized by the Holy Spirit that Lorenzo gave me upon my return in 1970. When I asked her about it, she related the following:

This was in October last year. I was feeling sick, and had not eaten anything. In fact, I felt so weak that in church I stayed on my chair instead of kneeling down when we prayed. I prayed, though, and afterward I felt very tired, and yet at the same time I felt strong enough to go to the altar and kneel down. *Hermano* Lorenzo said that I had spoken in tongues, and that this is how people felt afterward. It has not happened again.

[5] The self-reporting, and thus the cultural dogma, of the ethnographic informant is of paramount importance here, since not even an analysis of brain-wave patterns (EEG) could determine whether hypoarousal (meditative trance) or sleep is present: either may be accompanied by alpha waves.

Despite the great value attached to the behavior within her belief system, she seemed to accord little importance to what had happened, perhaps because she remembered absolutely nothing about it, only that afterward she felt stronger. That instead of slipping into sleep she went into trance may have been due mainly to the fact that a prayer was going on and not a sermon. Glossolalia is (culturally) expected at this time.

During the introductory phases of sleep people are generally immobile, but there is a great deal of body and eye movement during sleep itself. There is kinetic behavior, i.e., movement, during hyperarousal dissociation, but it is qualitatively quite different from the erratic, intermittent pattern we achieve within an eight-hour sleep period. Some people remain almost rigid, with only an occasional shiver, one or both hands clenched very tightly, or, as I saw in one case, "this *hermano* bends down so deeply [from a kneeling position] that his head nearly touches the floor. His palms are resting on the floor, but his thumbs are bent rigidly upward and back." There may be trembling, shaking, and twitching of face, thorax, or trunk; fingers cramping and stretching, hands fluttering, or performing other motions; in a kneeling position, the trunk may be thrown from side to side; there may be bowing, or rocking up and down or back and forth parallel to the ground; people may jump up and down from a kneeling position (seemingly while keeping their knees flexed), or, while standing, raise themselves to their toes. This motor behavior continues on into the vocalization, and the observational data indicate that the two aspects interact. This will be taken up later, together with the fact that some of the motor behavior is strictly rhythmical, some of it quite arhythmical, which has considerable functional significance.

Finally, that people wake from sleep is also true of the altered state: after a while, the subjects return to consciousness. Some do this spontaneously. The behavior pattern has run its course; they open their eyes, look a bit disoriented sometimes, as if lost, then go back to what they may have been doing just before achieving the trance, perhaps praying in ordinary language, preaching, singing, or even conversing (see Salvador's conversion story for the latter). Some people need a stimulus, a signal, a command, in order to return to ordinary behavior. This stimulus is admitted through the narrow channel that remains open during dissociation. In the congregations that I observed, the most customary of these signals was the ringing of a small bell having a rather high pitch.[6] It was rung either by the minister or by one of the *hermanos* in charge of that section of the service to indicate the termination of the altar call. The majority of those in trance wake at its sound, although others show a delayed response. And again, this part of the total pattern is subject to a great deal of individual variation, to be discussed in the chapter on waking.

INDUCTION OF HYPERAROUSAL DISSOCIATION

The question we naturally want to ask at this point is: how do people achieve this mental state, or how can it be induced? In discussing the problem, we must distinguish between the initial occurrence of the behavior and subsequent episodes.

Initially, first of all, some people may achieve dissociation spontaneously: no one needs to show it to them, they need have no inkling at all that it is possible. This demonstrates (as does its worldwide occurrence) that we are dealing with a capacity that is common to all men. I have an informant, for example, a young American woman from the Midwest, who attends only conservative church services (she is a Methodist) and, as far as she recalls, has never seen a person in trance, and yet, all of a sudden, she "just did it," went

6 The method is reminiscent of that of the hypnotist who claps his hands to bring his subject out of a hypnotic state. Similar mechanisms may, in fact, be involved. And yet a person in hyperarousal, as the ones observed here, behave very differently from the subjects of hypnotism. A state much more closely resembling hypnotism is that of *latah*, encountered in Southeast Asia, about which there is an extensive literature.

into dissociation. And what happened then bears out the contention that she was ignorant of the pattern usually seen in religious contexts: perhaps because her hobby was drawing and painting, she started drawing in this altered state of consciousness. We say she engaged—and still engages—in graphic automatisms, something the authors of occult literature call mediumistic writing (see Goodman 1971b for case histories and some of the relevant literature).

In many cases, of course, what looks like a spontaneous occurrence is not really that. A powerful conditioning factor is present, often out of awareness but still decisively affective. This factor, mentioned before, is cultural expectation. In a certain society, within a distinctly delineated situation, some particular person or all those present may expect to go into a trance. The instances of "spontaneous acquisition" of the behavior mentioned by our informants in their conversion stories, of "not knowing anything about it and yet it happened," are probably all in this class. The members of the various congregations are completely aware of this possibility. In the fall of 1969, for example, after I had left Utzpak, a boy wandered into the church and, upon seeing some *hermanos* going into glossolalia, also dissociated and produced a vocalization. He never came back to the church. The comment in the congregation was that this was not the real manifestation, it was not the Holy Spirit speaking with his tongue—he was "just doing it." Lorenzo had a different interpretation: the Lord had issued an invitation to the boy and, as a visible sign of this invitation, had placed his seal on him in the form of tongue-speaking. But the boy decided not to accept the call.

Not even the ethnographer is immune. In one of my first conversations with the minister in Utzpak, he said that of course he would like me to receive the blessing and the promise of the Holy Spirit while I was in Utzpak; he would pray for me when I was ready. "However," he continued, "the Spirit may come to you without either one of us actually asking for it." And he was right. This is what happened to me on my second Sunday there:

6 July, 1969. Sunday morning services, *matutin*, start
at six. I am up early enough to get up and dress, but
before I have a chance to light my gasoline stove, which
is still moist due to last night's heavy rain, Eusebia
[my informant] knocks. *"Kóʔoš, hermana"*—"Let's go."
I hastily swallow a raw egg, then grab my equipment,
and we leave.

In the church, Eusebia goes to kneel at the altar. The
last conscious memory I have of the episode to follow
is that of thinking, "At home when I was a child, we were
taught a little prayer to say before we sat down in church."
Then someplace in the church, I do not remember where,
I leaned against something, I do not know what. I saw
light, but then again I was surrounded by light, or perhaps
not, because the light was in me, and I was the light.
In this light I saw words in black outline—or were they
just letters?—descending upside down as if on a waterfall
of light. And at the same time I was full of a gaiety as if
my entire being were resounding with silver bells. Never
before had I ever felt this kind of luminous, ethereal,
delightful happiness.

I recovered with the thought: now I finally know what
joy is. I still don't remember where this was in the church,
I don't remember seeing Eusebia get back from the altar,
and in my original notebook I simply start recording,
"Sunday morning. Mother and sick child. Anselmo,
Valentin, and Lorenzo praying for him." [Unfortunately,
the few members of the congregation present at the time
were all at the altar and none had observed me.]

I am sure that it would be easy to find any number of
wage earners willing to testify that, although their alarm
did not go off and they had to rush out of the house without
breakfast, they did not go into dissociation upon arriving
at their desk. Yet I, at my place of work, did just that. I
think I was obeying a cultural expectation: I had seen demonstrated many times how people went into dissociation, I
was in the proper place at the proper time, thinking of
prayer, and then it happened to me, quite spontaneously
and without any conscious effort on my part. It did not
happen again because I intentionally blocked subsequent

occurrences. I needed at all times to be in complete command of all my faculties.

Second, people can be taught to go into trance. Actually, cultural expectation is already a part of this instruction. For this expectation is transmitted within the group and available to the newcomer either by way of demonstration or by word of mouth. Children are fascinated observers and never sent away. In the Cuarta Iglesia I even saw two small girls, both about four, not simply watching Salvador but also imitating his every movement. In one way or another most supplicants receive some preliminary information concerning such behavior, what happens and how it appears to the onlooker. It goes without saying that the powerful motivations set up for the glossolalia experience involve also the induction of dissociation, since it is recognized as a necessary first step, and the supplicants are made aware of this by word of mouth. This refers first of all to the conditions favoring the onset of the trance. Pastor Torres in Mexico City would emphasize, "Don't worry. Don't think about your life at home, your clothes, your food, your job. Concentrate only on receiving the Holy Spirit." Lorenzo speaks in a similar vein, but he also describes what it feels like to enter into an altered state. The Holy Spirit is like fire, he says, except that it does not consume, it only cleanses. It manifests itself in many forms; some people say they felt as if their heart had stopped, others felt heat, and one person he saw simply fell down as if in a faint.

Third, trance can be consciously induced. What is usually meant by this is that the individual can prepare mind and body for the trance state so that dissociation will invariably ensue, very much as when the plug is slipped into a wall outlet so that an electric motor will start running. It is my impression that there is something wrong with this concept. For instance, immobilized in a confined space, American subjects tend to hallucinate (hyperarousal), but Hoenig (1968) describes a Hatha Yoga subject who was buried and remained in meditative trance (hypoarousal). We need cross-cultural observations before we can make any general statement about a strategy *inevitably* resulting in this or that. For the time being, I feel, we should not say "induce" but rather "facilitate." The same holds true, for instance, for Neher's (1961) experiment on the auditory "driving" of ten volunteer subjects (they were exposed to drumbeat signals under controlled laboratory conditions). To be sure, their brains all showed a driving response. But the translation of this response into an altered state of consciousness is still a different matter, and is surely culturally conditioned.

As another example, Walter and Walter (1949) found that rhythmic sensory stimulation resulted in a number of behavioral effects in their subjects to which there was no counterpart in the respective stimuli. The following are these effects in order of seriousness:

1. visual: color, patterns, movement;
2. kinesthetic: swaying, spinning, jumping, vertigo;
3. cutaneous: tingling, pricking;
4. auditory perceptions;
5. visceral perceptions;
6. general emotional and abstract experience: fatigue, confusion, fear, disgust, anger, pleasure, disturbance of time sense;
7. organized hallucinations.

In other words, in essence, what happened with these subjects was quite similar to what was outlined for the persons in hyperarousal trance at the beginning of this chapter: there was a striking discrepancy between their manifest physical behavior as seen by the observer and the stimuli administered to them on the one hand, and what they subsequently reported about themselves on the other hand. Much of the agreement ends here, however. Subject to very similar stimuli, my informants' reports are quite dissimilar:

1. visual: only in one case did the subject see a descending light; quite generally, driving does not result in hallucination (with the possible exception of the perception of light when the behavior is achieved for the first time);
2. kinesthetic: the majority of the informants report floating only;

3. cutaneous: prickling is reported in one case;
4. there are no auditory perceptions reported as a result of driving;
5. visceral: of the viscera, only the heart's action is perceived (as speeding up); other parts of the body, however, are frequently mentioned, such as the head, tongue, chest, shoulders, small of the back, veins;
6. general emotional and abstract experience: the difference between the groups becomes especially striking in this area; fatigue, first in importance on the first list, is reported by only one of my informants, and even in this case the fatigue had been present before the trance experience, and was felt to be less after the episode. Confusion is registered by a number of informants, but only by facial expression: it is not perceived. Pleasure—if we can interpret this as euphoria—is reported by all Apostolic informants interviewed, as is a disturbance of the time sense, only sixth and seventh, respectively, on the Walter and Walter list.

The imperfect fit between the two sets of results is due, to my mind, to cultural patterning. This seems especially true with respect to general emotional and abstract experiences that show the greatest disparity, because probably subject to the most intense cultural permutation. Data from the anthropological literature tend to confirm this view. Schäfer (1950) describes the Tibetan state oracle, mentioned before, a high-ranking ecclesiastical official, as being totally exhausted after a hyperarousal trance and depressed to the point of believing that he will surely become ill and not live long due to this yearly ordeal. Dr. Bourguignon has pointed out to me that this is also the general tenor of the experience of Siberian shamans.

With these reservations in mind we are now ready to consider *driving*, the mechanism referred to several times above. Driving, basically, has to do with rhythm. Human behavior patterns are rhythmical: our heart beats at a regular rhythm, we breathe rhythmically, we also walk and speak that way. Some of these rhythms, however, are more amen-

able to conscious modifications than others. We can alter
the rhythm of our walk or, with effort, even make it very
unrhythmical; we can also hold our breath or change the
length of the phrases that we utter between two pauses.
Affecting our heartbeat is more difficult, but subjects versed
in Hatha Yoga and other Eastern disciplines certainly can
do so even if we cannot. Now: what seems to be aimed at,
implicitly at least, in driving as I have observed it is somehow
to produce dissociation by affecting these rhythms, that is,
those least amenable to conscious control such as brain
patterns, possibly by altering their shapes or interfering with
their base frequency—making them faster or slower. Perhaps the action involves certain neurological centers in a
rhythmical pattern in which they ordinarily do not participate, or in a contrary action barring them from participation where they usually would do so, all by this enforced,
superimposed rhythmical stimulus. What really happens no
one as yet seems to know. Neurophysiologists are familiar
with some brain wave patterns produced by photic driving
(regular flashing of light) in a small number of psychiatric
patients, and Neher (1961) published parallel data on acoustic driving (drumbeat) in normal subjects. Some preliminary
findings by Palmer (1966) on subjects in glossolalia will be
discussed later. But this is a very incomplete picture. We
know nothing at all, for example, about changes in pulse
rate or brain wave patterns (EEGs) during the various
phases of this mental state.[7] All we know is that, under very
specific conditions, conscious cortical control is actually lost.
The person, that is, the conscious self (*rejtőzik,* as the
Hungarian shamans say) goes into hiding, so to speak.

Certain preliminary measures make it easier for the body
to react to driving. Drugs may be employed that may even
make driving superfluous, but this strategy is not used by
the congregations I studied. And yet they all understood
that fasting will facilitate the achievement of a trance.

---

[7] Except perhaps by inference. See Darmadji and Pfeiffer (1969),
referred to in chap. 6.

Fasting has important biochemical consequences, among others a lowering of the blood-sugar level, which in turn can affect consciousness. A field observation may serve to illustrate the same point. When I came to Utzpak in 1969, not a single woman had spoken in tongues in the ten-year history of the congregation. In the manner in which the women participated in the life of the congregation, it was quite clear that they considered religious activity an exclusively masculine concern. None of the women, for instance, offered a special hymn or testimony. Lorenzo from the start of his ministry in Utzpak disregarded these attitudes or possibly was unaware of them. He formed a chapter of the national women's organization of the Apostolic church, called "Dorcas," where until then there had been only a chapter of the men's organization (Señores cristianos). And while emphasizing that women could not preach, he demanded their active participation in all other aspects of the service. Under his prompting, Francisca, and after her Chela and Anita, achieved the behavior, the only ones who were breast-feeding at the time. It is my contention that it was this lactation, in addition to fasting, that on the biochemical level helped them to overcome their culturally prefigured inhibition about breaking into the male domain, and aided them in initiating the glossolalia behavior. As could be predicted, subsequent female glossolalia followed easily: other women were taught more readily by demonstration since, culturally, the behavior had been incorporated.

In addition, other biochemical mechanisms may be involved. As shown in Table 1, some of the manifest behavior points to a parasympathetic agent being activated by the body, others to a sympathetic agent (i.e., as though a compound were involved that acts in the same manner as the parasympathetic or sympathetic part of the autonomic nervous system respectively). Some German researchers (Wiechert and Göllnitz 1969) found in rat experiments that during cerebral convulsions there was an increase in the activity of glutaminase and glutamine synthetase as well as in the level of free ammonia in the brain. What the be-

TABLE 1

BIOCHEMISTRY OF AROUSAL

(After Gardner 1963:211; as against field data on *Apostolicos,* last column)

(Functions of the autonomic nervous system) Organ	Parasym-pathetic	Sympa-thetic	Hyperarousal (occurrence in)
Lacrimal, nasal, palatine, and salivary glands	+	−	+
Alimentary canal	+	−	vomiting?
Peripheral blood vessels	− (no effect)	+ (con-striction and dila-tion)	+ (dilation, but not in eyeballs)
Sweat glands and smooth muscle of skin	− (no effect)	+ (sweat-ing, erec-tion of hair)	+ (pre-dominantly sweating)

+ = stimulation   − = inhibition

havioral correlates might be of such a biochemical event, if it takes place at all in humans, we cannot possibly postulate at this time.

On the other hand, physical effort such as that involved in heavy labor inhibits the capability of those who wish to go into a trance. Often it prevents a trance from occurring entirely. In Utzpak, this was very clear after the men all cooperated in rebuilding the church roof (1969) and again after piling an *albarrada,* a wall of limestone rocks, around the church property (1970).

Driving in the Apostolic congregations takes place in three stages. The first, preliminary one consists in singing hymns with very clear, relatively rapid beats and clapping to the rhythm of the singing. The effect of this introductory behavior is enhanced by the musical instruments accompanying the singing and continuing in some churches (Hammond, Mexico City) into the altar call. In the second stage, the supplicant is prayed for by other members of the con-

gregation and the minister, serving as instructors, usually
very loudly and also in a strongly accented pattern in some
instances, and this prayer soon merges into the glossolalia
pattern of the instructors, which is now in a third stage, also
being shouted at the supplicant. The limits between the three
stages are quite fluid, especially between the second and the
third. In addition to this driving on the rhythmical level,
there are some totally unrhythmical patterns that for some
reason seem to facilitate the entrance into the trance and
later, after the trance has been established, apparently en-
hance the state or even drive it to higher peaks. (More about
this later, p. 132.) Such are unrhythmical walking (Hammond) and clapping in obvious arhythmical patterns as well
as arhythmical manipulation of the body. In the latter, the
minister places his hands on the head of the supplicant,
shaking it lightly, even applying some pressure, or manipu-
lates the rib cage in the same manner.

The following is a description of the pertinent parts of a
service especially dedicated to the prayer for the Holy Spirit,
which in Utzpak takes place every Sunday morning. A few
observations made at other services are added in brackets.

29 June, 1969. Sunday morning service [*matutin*].
After the usual introductory part consisting of hymns,
prayers, Bible reading, Lorenzo gives his sermon. He directs
it mostly to the manifestation of the Holy Spirit. Before
he himself had the manifestation of speaking in tongues,
he was full of doubts. Maybe what people said was true,
maybe it was not. But after he himself had spoken in
tongues, he had no more doubts. [Other points he makes
during sermons introducing the prayer for the Holy Spirit:
Without the Holy Spirit, people get cold, they are easily
brainwashed, and even are lost. Without having the
Holy Spirit to help him, the minister would go to sleep,
it is the Holy Spirit that impulses him. When you pray
for the Holy Spirit, you should leave all other thoughts
behind: problems in your home, in your work; the women
should not think about whether there is food in the house,
or what they might want to shop for. Also one should not
be worried about how he might act when the Holy Spirit

takes over. Some people hit about them, or they jump;
these are supernatural manifestations. A change in language
is the natural thing to happen. Some people get scared
when they feel that something supernatural is beginning
to happen to them, but they should let go, they should
let it happen.]

There is a hymn, then a prayer in which glossolalia
already occurs. Emilo is speaking in tongues; the upper part
of his body goes forward and back while in kneeling position.
Lorenzo is also in glossolalia; he rocks back and forth
on palms and knees. Xavier is very audible; he puts his
hands behind his neck, then releases them and holds one
upward, letting the other arm drop.

Lorenzo now preaches again, once more about speaking
in tongues. If you feel like shouting, shout. That is noisy,
but we have this service in the daytime for that reason.
He then gives exact orders on how to proceed with the
prayer. Those that desire the Holy Spirit are to kneel next
to the rostrum. Those that already have received it kneel
behind them. He points to the precise positions to be
occupied. Those who wish to receive the Holy Spirit
are to repeat, "séllame, séllame" ["seal me"], nothing else.
When they feel that their language is changing, they should
not get scared and stop, and just cry, like some people.
For it is the change in language that constitutes the
manifestation of the Holy Spirit. They should continue,
for now God speaks through them and no one knows in
what language. Those that have already had the
manifestation are to say only "séllalos, séllalos, séllalos"
["seal them"], nothing else. If they want to say something
different in prayer, they should resist the wish. If, of course,
their language should change, then they should obey and
let the Holy Spirit take over.

While singing the hymn "Santo Espíritu descende"
[Descend, Holy Spirit] and then passing over into the
rousing corito, "Fuego, fuego, fuego es que quiero: dámelo,
dámelo, dámelo Señor" [It is fire that I want; give it to me,
oh Lord], the congregation kneels down. Lorenzo has not
assigned any place to the women. No woman has ever had
the manifestation in this congregation. But Eusebia goes
slowly up to the women's side of the altar, closes the window

there, and kneels down. Beside her are Francisca and
Anita, both with infants in their arms. There is a prayer
in ordinary language for the Spirit to manifest itself, then
begins the *"séllame, séllame"* and *"séllalos, séllalos"* in an
accelerating tempo. The men who have had the experience
before keep going into glossolalia, then coming out again, as
evidenced by ordinary-language utterances. Lorenzo walks
in and out among those kneeling, sometimes with difficulty
because there is tendency for them to draw closer to each
other in dissociation. He is often in glossolalia and shouts
it at them, seeming to drive them to ever greater effort.
He bends down to Felipe, shouting his glossolalia almost
into his ear [often punctuating its rhythm with an up-and-
down, equally rhythmical, motion of his fist]. He lays on
hands, shaking the supplicants' head or their chest.
There are discernable peaks in the various glossolalias,
and then dropping levels, in some instances with return
to *"séllalos."* Finally the activity abates, the men wipe
their faces. Waking is instantaneous, except for Felipe,
who sits on the *marimbol*, still shaking slightly. A *corito* is
intoned, then Lorenzo starts speaking, pale, perfectly calm
face, even voice. He says that if any one of the people
present would like to pray at their own home, in private,
rather than at the service, he will be glad to go with them.
Then he asks if any one of the men praying for the
manifestation already felt "something." Anselmo and
Felipe answer in the affirmative. He suggests that they
continue praying. They should continually say *"séllame,"*
and if their tongue refuses to say this Spanish word any
more, then they should let it happen, even if it comes
out stuttering—God often speaks through people in this
way. Felipe cannot formulate exactly what he felt,
but knows it was something.

   Lorenzo calls for a hymn, then once more orders the
same arrangement as before. The three glossolalists and
Lorenzo as well as Xavier very quickly pass from *"séllalos"*
into glossolalia. Emilio, especially, is striking. His tears
are flowing, there is some salivation, a tremendous amount
of perspiration. Of the prospective glossolalists, Felipe
is once more in trance, his arms shaking. Anselmo is
clapping, and his *"séllame"* gradually passes into a com-

pressed shout, strange for a man who has a rather high
tenor voice. Felipe is now on palms and knees. I cannot
hear his glossolalia, but Lorenzo is bending down to him,
putting his hands on his head, then bending down and
listening. He passes in turn to each of the other prospective
glossolalists, often in glossolalia himself, with slightly
upturned face, closed eyes, perspiration thick on his face.
The noise level is deafening. And yet there are islands of
quietude. Pedro [Licha's husband] and his father pray
very quietly next to each other. Licha wanders in and out,
Reinita in her arms or at her breast. Eusebia is standing
absolutely motionless at the altar.

Finally, Xavier gets up. The praying becomes very quiet.
Anselmo, who is still on his knees, clapping like an
automaton, stops when Xavier lightly taps his back.
Everybody is wet with perspiration. Eusebia goes to her
seat, so do Isaía, Pedro, and his father. Xavier is now at
the extreme left of the rostrum, Emilio and Floriano on
the extreme right, Lorenzo behind the rostrum. Anselmo
and Felipe kneel somewhat farther back, closer to the
congregation. Xavier and Emilio once more go into
glossolalia. Lorenzo gets up, rings the bell. The glossolalia
immediately stops. They all go to their seats, remain
standing, wiping their faces. Eusebia opens the window,
and Lorenzo asks everybody to sit down. He is pale now,
his usual color, and very quiet and commonplace. He asks
for testimony about the experience of the Holy Spirit.
Anselmo comes forward, faces the congregation. He speaks
a few generalities, that he is happy to have had the joy
[el gozo] of the Lord.

Felipe comes forth next, also speaks of the joy in the
Lord, but when the pastor asks him whether he thinks
he has had the manifestation of the Holy Spirit, he hesitates
and says that he is not sure. Lorenzo's somewhat annoyed
comment: "But of course he has had it, I myself have
heard it, I don't know why he now doesn't want to say it.
He had a very strong manifestation, and his language
changed, and that precisely is the sign. Some," he
continues, "keep saying that they have not as yet had the
manifestation when in fact they have had it. I recall two
sisters in Chetumal who maintained the same thing. The

sign is the change in language; when that happens, that
is the sign, and their language did change. I don't know
what else they expected! You feel heat, you think you are
here no longer, and then your language changes."

One of the *hermanos* who did not receive the manifestation comes forth. He felt nothing, he says. Perhaps he has
a hard heart. He needs more prayer.

Quite ceremoniously, Lorenzo now records in his
churchbook that on Sunday, 29 June, 1969 Felipe and
Anselmo were baptized by the Holy Spirit.

The glossolalia behavior proper as well as the waking,
both alluded to in the above observation, will be taken up
in respective chapters. I present them here in order to keep
intact the total event.

A strategy for inducing hyperarousal dissociation that
does not involve driving should be mentioned briefly. It is
hyperventilation. There is evidence of it on the Umbanda
tapes, to be discussed in the next chapter. Among the
Apostolicos I observed it only once, in 1970, in an episode
mentioned earlier in this chapter (p. 61). In this instance it
may have represented an independent invention stimulated
by the mounting excitement in the week preceding the
baptism. In four minutes, hyperventilation (rapid, deep
breathing) will eliminate half of the readily available carbon
dioxide in the various soft tissues of the body, including
the brain (Stoddard 1967:80). This produces a drastic
change in the acid-base balance of the brain, a shift in
hydrogen ion concentration toward the alkaline side, and,
even with a much shorter breathing time, will lead to convulsions and disturbances in consciousness.

We have now seen how a hyperarousal trance is established for the first time, how, that is, the behavior is transmitted, learned, acquired. Subsequent episodes are initiated
with relative ease, as indicated by the observations reported
here. The same was also seen by other researchers such as
Pattison (1968 and personal communication) and Pfeiffer
(1968). The latter remarks: "Es ist anzunehmen, dass häufig
wiederholte Trance zu einer Labilität des Bewusstseins

führt and dass die Umschaltung nach Art eines bedingten Reflexes schon durch geringe Reize ausgelöst werden kann" (p. 12).[8] The future glossolalist has learned to go into dissociation and, by whatever means, he has set up a patterning in the neurophysiological circuits. Later events can now be called up by a variety of stimuli.

In discussing the onset of renewed episodes, however, we will have to distinguish between laity and the clergy. The laity relies, apparently, mostly on situational control. Aside from preparation by preliminary strategies such as fasting, singing and rhythmic clapping, kneeling, and praying loudly, the manifestation is simply viewed as a natural adjunct of worshipful behavior and is accepted as it comes. It is expected, and it happens. The clergy, however, is aware of possible control. As Felipe, one of the ministers of the Utzpak congregation, puts it: "I am now able to speak in tongues; when I want to, I can control it, and if I don't want to, then I can contain myself. I can also control whether I speak loudly or quietly." When I asked Lorenzo whether he could also control it, he said he could, but only to a certain extent. He was the only one of the ministers I had the occasion to observe over an extended period, and I tried to discover in what way this control takes place and what might be its limitations. (In the following discussion, for reasons to be discussed in the next chapter, I am taking the appearance of the glossolalia to be diagnostic for the onset of the dissociation.)

One of the most obvious mechanisms Lorenzo employs is that of trigger words such as, for example, *obra*—work, your miracle, that is. He calls out "*Obra, obra, Señor, obra,*" and at that continues in glossolalia. (In October 1969, Dr. Julius Laffal, of the Connecticut Valley Hospital, informed me of a study of his with a speaker who had, as he wrote, "rather remarkable control over his glossolalia speech, and responded to specific stimulus words which had been agreed

[8] "It is to be assumed that frequently repeated trances lead to a lability of consciousness, and that a switch-over may be triggered even by minimal stimuli in the manner of a conditioned reflex."

upon in interviews with brief flows of glossolalia.") This is
much the same procedure as when we remember a poem if
someone will give us the first line. But in glossolalia more
automatism is involved than in the conscious state. For
instance, on one occasion, later the same day, Lorenzo was
in the midst of his sermon. In context, he used the word
obra, went into a brief glossolalia phrase, and a lost look
appeared on his face. There was a small, awkward pause.
He said "*Bendito sea Dios*" ["Blessed be the Lord"], which
fits just about anywhere, and then continued his sermon.
In other words, while *obra* does call up the glossolalia, it
might also do so inadvertently, in a context where such a
result is not sought.

In the course of the summer, however, the number of
observed trigger words increased. There were, in addition
to *obra* (work) and *poder* (power), *aleluya*, *misericordia*, and
others.

I am getting worried about this trigger-word mechanism.
I can see that it is actually operative in many instances,
but the list is getting too long. There must be also a
different mode, possibly connected with certain "loaded"
words only indirectly. Then I witness a spontaneous
triggering. The congregation has a visitor, *Hermano*
Peregrino from Chetumal, who brings a gift from that
group of sixty-nine pesos, which he makes an even seventy
from his own pocket. The gift is earmarked for improve-
ments on the church. This will put a roof over Lorenzo's
head, whose wife will give birth soon to their second child.
The *casa pastoral*, separated from the church proper
by a man-high wall but within the same structure, has
a mud floor and is uninhabitable because of the leaks in
the tarpaper. Lorenzo calls for a prayer for the offering,
so that the givers may receive multiple compensation for
their generosity. Almost immediately, there is what sounds
like a catch in his throat, and without any of the trigger
words I am already familiar with, he goes into glossolalia.

This observation, I think, pinpoints a second mechanism:
certain contexts, often possibly tied stereotypically to par-

ticular words, produce an emotional arousal, which in turn leads to the trance and glossolalia. This might be the path by which the utterance was produced that interrupted Salvador's conversion story.

Not only trigger words and emotional complexes but apparently also behavior patterns can call up the dissociation. We mentioned Nicolas's manipulation of his guitar. Another example appears in the following observation. As reported earlier, one of the manipulations the would-be trancer is subjected to is shaking his head. In an unrelated situation, that of blessing a kneeling couple who had invited the congregation to hold a service in their house, Lorenzo laid his hands on the man's head. "Suddenly, he goes into a very steeply rising glossolalia, while pressing the man's head and shaking it. Simultaneously, he breaks out into profuse perspiration."

In the next chapter we will discuss the glossolalia utterance, superimposed as it is upon the substratum of the hyperarousal dissociation like the roofcomb on the top of a Mayan temple.

4 The Glossolalia Utterance

In earlier chapters we have seen how the expectation about speaking in tongues is set up: first of all, there is the central, oft-repeated tenet that achieving it is of utmost religious importance. It is one unit of an eschatological dyad, but it is the more important of the two, representing the promise of eternal life. Together with baptism by water it constitutes the entrance ticket to heaven—or, upon the Second Coming, into the Kingdom of God: water washes away the sins, and speaking in tongues is a manifestation of the Holy Spirit. But while water baptism not followed by glossolalia is felt to be an opportunity lost, great anxiety arises if a person speaks in tongues and has not yet been baptized by immersion. Such persons, although "very close to God," are in grave ritual danger, from which only water baptism can save them. The anthropologist is familiar with this kind of anxiety attendant upon contact with what is thought to be divine in the belief systems of many societies. In the present congregations, viewed on a scale of intensity, its weakest representation is in the Hammond congregation, its peak in Yucatán, with the Cuarta Iglesia of Mexico City occupying an intermediary position.

If glossolalia does not ensue, people are admonished to continue to pray, to fast, not to resist. It may be occasion for disappointment, as in the case of Lorenzo—his companion was singled out for this show of grace, while he only perspired and cried and felt hot—or for fear, as in Utzpak, where some members of the congregation are convinced that a trance without glossolalia signifies that Satan is trying to get hold of the person. The trance is only valued as a recognizable first step toward glossolalia.

In this connection I observed an interesting, because so obviously culturally structured, difference between the Hammond congregation and the ones in Mexico (including Yucatán). In the Hammond church, I saw an elderly man, a young woman, and a boy in dissociation simultaneously, during the same service. But while the man was surrounded by some of the other men, trying to drive him into glossolalia, and the woman was being helped on by two other women, no one paid any attention to the boy, who was visibly in dissociation, his eyes tightly closed, slowly spinning on his toes, with his arms extended and flapping in a slow rhythm. In Utzpak all efforts are immediately concentrated on the trancer, whether in his early teens (they can become members of the juvenile section at fourteen) or at any other age beyond that, and the same is true of all the other Apostolic congregations I became acquainted with in Mexico. In other words, teenagers in these congregations are not relegated to an intermediate position between childhood and adult status as they are with us, and neither are they in the Mexican or Yucatecan urban or rural societies.

That the trance rather than the subsequent vocalization behavior could be the real locus for the conversion experience is rarely maintained, and in this respect Gregoria and her son Nicolas are the exceptions, not just among the ten whose conversion stories are described in the previous chapter, but quite generally.

Teaching and induction techniques also explicitly aim at producing the step into vocalization and only incidentally result in dissociation as the first phase.

Second, both the laity and the clergy recognize the significance of the behavior as cementing the congregation: it is the single most powerful cohesive factor of the group. To drive yet another supplicant into the manifestation is a constantly reenacted communal effort. It is this behavior also that sets off the congregation from the community at large and from both the Catholic and the other Protestant groups. Derision by the ambient society, charges of insanity, and witchcraft, all due to trance behavior, strengthen group solidarity.

Finally the rewards are great for the individual. He is taught to expect reassurance: "It gives a feeling of security to receive the manifestation of the Holy Spirit," Lorenzo says in one of his sermons. "We know what we have." And echoing the sentiment, Eusebia states, "With the *Apostolicos*, there is certainty." From others who have already spoken in tongues, the parishioner hears of the aftereffects of carefree joy and hope, and from participating in the life of the congregation he is aware of the standing, the prestige the behavior brings in its wake. All in all, the positive content of the anticipation is as potent as it is complex.

Beyond the above ideational orientation there is also specific conditioning aimed at reassuring the supplicant that speaking in tongues is indeed possible. This is carried out both by word of mouth and by demonstration, in the sermons and the altar calls respectively. The latter are part of every service and nearly always feature glossolalia. (In the laboratory, Cohn's volunteers achieved vocalization with the help of similar preparation: "It was suggested to them that speaking in tongues is possible, and the phenomenon was observed by most of them in Pentecostal churches" [1968: 278]).

It is indicative of the difficulty of achieving the vocalization step on the substratum of the dissociation that, despite all this comprehensive indoctrination, so many of those seeking the manifestation are so slow in acquiring it. To be sure, as some of our conversion accounts given earlier and additional examples indicate, vocalization can and does occur spontaneously. But for most the step is a hard learning task, the reason being that learning is a process that requires the calling up of a host of mental faculties, among them awareness, focusing of attention, desire for verification, and memory, all of which are diminished or possibly not available at all in hyperarousal dissociation. It is not unlike being trained in tightrope walking with one's eyes taped shut. An observation made in August 1969 in the Cuarta Iglesia will illustrate this point. This was a service conducted by Juan D. L. in the absence of the pastor.

At the first altar call I note a young man standing almost directly in front of me. The room serving as church while the new building is being constructed is rather small, so the usual separation into the women's side and the men's side cannot be observed. Juan prays standing, behind the rostrum, and everyone else around me does it that way too—there is practically no room to kneel down. The man before me is beginning to shiver, then shakes still more strongly, but there is no glossolalia.

During the second altar call, there is a curious interplay between the young man and Juan. He begins shaking as Juan goes into dissociation. Juan claps, he claps. Juan gives a brief glossolalia utterance, the man remains silent, only shaking more strongly. Juan uses some arhythmical clapping to drive himself into renewed glossolalia effort, the man gives nearly the identical clapping pattern. Juan is in glossolalia again, the man claps very hard and fast; now Juan is out, the man shivers, but his jaws are definitely not moving. The whole scene is a double play, with Juan in intermittent glossolalia, and the other man being moved along, as if on a string, but in complete silence.

What is going on here, to my mind, is that, without some acoustic driving directly oriented upon him, the supplicant is unable to accomplish the step into vocalization. In all probability, the instruction he took along into dissociation was something like this: watch the deacon, he will guide you. Thus, he was able to pick up the deacon's kinetic behavior, although in dissociation. But Juan's glossolalia utterances in this instance were brief, rather low in intensity and volume, and, particularly, they were not beamed directly at the supplicant. The "channel" we spoke about in the previous chapter was clearly not permeable for such a weak, diffuse signal.

How, then, is vocalization behavior learned? The most effective strategy is the acoustic driving of the supplicant,

but not all the congregations I observed are equally aware
of this. In Hammond, for instance, I observed a young
woman in considerable dissociation, who was staggering a
few steps this way and that, accompanied and gently guided
away from obstructing chairs by two other women, who
encouraged her in normal speech—"Jesus wants you: open
your mouth. He wants to talk through your mouth. Let him
come to you," and so on—and then alternately, shouted
their glossolalia at her. In the Cuarta Iglesia, the preliminary
indoctrination in the sermons is quite intense, but acoustic
driving is diffuse at best, with the congregation kneeling at
the altar and the supplicant seeking the manifestation having to exert a great deal of volition to tune in, as it were, on
what glossolalia there is going on around him.

Not so in the Mérida congregation, where I saw *Hermano*
Manuel, for example, standing beside a man who was trying
to achieve vocalization; he was shouting his own glossolalia
at him again and again slipping into dissociation and jumping up and down, thus emphasizing his vocal pattern. In
Mérida, however, just as in the congregation in Mexico City,
those seeking the manifestation kneel scattered among the
other parishioners and are not subject to the concerted
effort of a group.

In Utzpak, finally, the subject is affected both by group
and individual driving. His guides kneel around him in a
semicircle (see Fig. 1), shouting "*séllalo, séllalo*," and soon

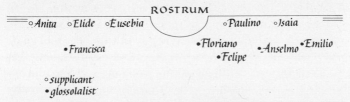

Fig. 1. Kneeling arrangement during prayer for the Holy
Spirit in Utzpak, Yucatán, Summer 1969.

their own glossolalia (only those are asked to participate in
this arrangement who have already mastered the step into
glossolalia); and the pastor also directs his own driving

directly at him in the same kind of pattern of slipping in and
out of dissociation as seen in Hammond and in Mérida
(see above):

Lorenzo concentrates on Tacho who, not yet in
vocalization, is trembling and rocking on his knees, and
drives him with his own glossolalia. What I mean by that
is, he bends down to him, shouts his own glossolalia almost
into his ear, often punctuating its rhythm with an
up-and-down motion of his fist. Now he is back with
Anita, shakes her head with both hands, drives her higher
with his own glossolalia, as if the intention were to intensify
her dissociation to the utmost of her capacity. [The
minister's dissociation is light in such instances, but still
easily observable.]

This composite teaching strategy is by far the most effective I have had a chance to observe. By the summer of
1970 it had been abandoned for various reasons (including
an increase in membership, so that there was very little
room during altar calls, and the progressive loss of interest
of the minister; see his conversion story), and the pattern
reverted to that seen in Mérida.

In summary then, a comparison of the various congregations shows that the more concerted the effort, the sooner is
the desired result attained. In Hammond, only immediate
associates are involved in a relatively easygoing driving,
and the returns are low. In the Cuarta and in Mérida, both
the congregation and the ministers and their helpers drive,
but there is something about the spatial arrangements that
cuts down its intensity. Dispersed as the supplicants are
among others in the congregation, all praying, to be sure,
but some in ordinary language, some in tongues, some directing their prayer directly at them, some not, the effect is
diffuse. In Utzpak, with the supporters of the supplicant
arranged in a semicircle around him, and very close, and
all of them involved in the same rhythmical driving pattern
of the deafening "*séllalo, séllalo*," a favorable result is almost a foregone conclusion.

As to the acoustic signals now, both meaningful utterances and glossolalia are equally beamed at the supplicant: see the above example cited from Hammond. Or from Mérida: "Manuel jumps up and down, now also clapping, and keeps shouting '*séllalo, séllalo*,' and '*Gloria Cristo*.' He goes in and out of glossolalia." Yet observation shows that, in dissociation, the supplicant picks up only the glossolalia utterance. What happens, I think, is that when the supplicant is in a conscious state the glossolalia is screened out and is not identified as the manifestation sought.

Nohoč Felipe, Eusebia's husband, comes in from the jungle with the firewood for the day in his tumpline [pack sling]. He wants to hear how yesterday's *coritos* and hymns sound on the tape recorder. In playing them back to him, I come to a section containing the glossolalias of himself and of Floriano. Lorenzo also comes in [he is temporarily housed in Eusebia's home, since the roof of the *casa pastoral* leaks] and stops to listen. When I get to the glossolalia section, Lorenzo says, "*What* is *that?*" Felipe has no idea either. The fidelity of the tape recorder is quite good, and these people immediately recognize each other's voice, even in singing, or if there is only a word or so audible. Not even Lorenzo, whose dissociation rarely seems very intense, recognizes either himself or the glossolalia of the others.

This screening is not effective in dissociation. In fact, some of the instructions given may even work expressly to exclude ordinary language, directing attention, in the contrary sense, to what is *not* meaningful speech.

They should continually say, "*séllame, séllame*," Lorenzo tells his congregation, and if their tongue refuses to say this Spanish word any more, they should let it happen, even if it comes out stuttering—God often speaks through people in this way.

Finally, the supplicant's efforts are successful and he actually begins "speaking in tongues." In some, the transition from language to dissociative vocalization is hard to note. The meaningful speech slowly dissolves, as if wiped away, and the patterns of glossolalia take over. In others, the first vocalization event is truly dramatic. Over and over in my field notes, I find the description, "he *breaks* into vocalization." It is as if a tremendous wall were being rent apart, some weighty obstacle literally blown up, a neurophysiological breach established that was not available before. Generally speaking, vocalization in the conscious state is already an energy discharge mechanism (Laffal 1965, 1967). This is also the case in dissociation, but apparently in this state there is such a barrage directed against whatever occlusion there is in the path of access to the speech centers to enable this discharge of energy to take place that the first vocalization may be nothing more than a compressed shout. This is then followed by an utterance of tremendous pulse frequency. In Hammond, for example, a woman seemed to have a violent attack of chattering teeth while trying to say [uː]; in the Cuarta the occlusion of a woman observed in such an utterance was at the level of the glottis so that the resulting vocalization was a [ʔu ʔu ʔu ʔu] of equal speed; and among the Maya speakers both men and women on occasion evidenced the same pattern. At somewhat decreased energy, there may be an exceedingly large frequency of lower-effort consonants and vowels (see Fig. 3, p. 106), again observed both in Saint Vincent and in Utzpak with Maya speakers.[1]

Depending on the individual, this high-energy vocalization will persist for varying lengths of time, eventually giving way to a stereotypy on a somewhat reduced level. While the above type of utterance seems predominantly physiology-produced, the subsequent stereotypy is model-oriented. Its vocal content is fixed, not necessarily in the

[1] The question concerning the relationship between the speaker's native phone inventory and his glossolalia is a complex one and will be taken up elsewhere. Bryant and O'Connell (1971) found a remarkably low correlation between the glossolalia and normal utterances of English speakers, due principally, however, to a variation in vowel frequency.

same mold as that of the minister but of whoever happened to be the guide who led the way into glossolalia. Thus in the Cuarta there was the stable [siø:] of Juan, which was reflected in the other speakers; in Utzpak, Lorenzo mirrored Gilberto (as did the latter's mother, Gregoria, and brother, Nicolas), while his utterance in turn, and in approximation, was reproduced by Anselmo, Isaía, Cilia, Nesto, and many others of the congregation. On the other hand, in Mérida a young girl was singing in dissociation in a melody line very similar to that of Gregoria who had guided her. Yet none of the pulse configurations (series of "syllables" heard in an utterance) of this level, that is of the level reached by the speaker when the great initial push has worn off and a certain stereotypy has been reached, which I observed in Hammond, ever turned up in the Mexico City church. We may thus conclude that the significance of that visit may have been mostly a demonstration of a greater abandon, a more significant lack of inhibition than customarily prevails in the Mexican congregation. The pulse inventory (i.e., the "syllables" heard by the observer) then represents a kind of record of who the guide was who led the particular glossolalist into the behavior, in addition to demonstrating in which congregation he achieved his stereotypy; in other words, his personal vocalization history.

In addition, the character of the utterance also indicates the state at which the individual happens to be with respect to the behavior. As I mentioned, it was one of the great surprises of this investigation, as I observed the glossolalia in the same speakers over a two-year, and in some instances over a three-year, period, when I realized that the character of their utterance changed. To my mind, this observation offers an explanation for some of the many disparities in the observational data in the literature. For instance, Palmer (1966) never thought to ask his subjects how long they had been speaking in tongues but assumed, apparently, that the behavior, once acquired, remained constant. Yet my data show, within the time of observation, a considerable decline in the energy content discharged. This is perceived in a decrease in loudness, intensity, and difference in pitch between the lowest and the highest point of the curve (of which more later in this chapter) as well as in the disappearance of the majority of the high-effort vowels ([i, u]), with others such as [a,ə] taking their place. There is also an increase in the variety of pulses, the duration of the individual utterance becomes progressively longer, and the total episode tends to shrink. (These various terms will be discussed later, in connection with the individual utterances to be presented.) The stereotypy, in other words, does not really produce a stable system of automatisms.

During stereotypy, a more or less tenuous bond is established between the vocalization and the hyperaroused state. In other words, when a person goes into dissociation he will also utter glossolalia. I want to contend that, conversely, when he utters glossolalia, he is also in hyperarousal. There is considerable argument on this point, with some researchers contending that no dissociation, no trance, is present at all (e.g., Samarin 1968), or that the behavior is faked (Calley 1965), or is present only occasionally (Hine 1969). All this disagreement hinges, to my mind, on the fact that the diagnostic signals of the altered state were not known and the evolution over time of the behavior had not before been noted. While initially the dissociation and the vocalization occur consecutively, at least in most cases, the interval between the former and latter may become contracted to the point where they seem to occur simultaneously. Concurrently, the dissociation may become very light. The diagnostic signals such as tightly closed eyes, perspiration, tears, and flushing may not all be present. There may be nothing more than lightly closed eyes and a faint shudder, only weak traces of once-vigorous behavior. The observer who has not been alerted to the diagnostic symptoms may easily overlook them. He will also neglect to pick up certain linguistic clues, should the subject utter intelligible words (which, as we shall see, may also happen) such as an unexpected lengthening of certain syllables, a catch in the throat, and so on. To summarize, I propose that the glossolalia behavior, established as it is on the substratum of the altered state of consciousness, remains, for the duration of the behavior, tied to this substratum. The altered state is established first, but whether it also endures longer I cannot tell at this point in my research. I have some indication that it may prove the more permanently available of the two intertwining behaviors.

As mentioned earlier, during the phase of stereotypy the pulse inventory is fixed, it does not vary. This is what stereotypy in this context means: the subject keeps saying the same thing, the utterance does not vary from one occasion to the next. Instead of saying that the utterance is stereotyped, we might state that it is remembered. In the waking state, however, the glossolalist often does not remember that he spoke; he does not recall, when out of dissociation, what he said, and no subject I interviewed could repeat his trance utterance in the conscious state. Also, and this may be quite significant, no glossolalist among my informants ever said that he *heard* himself.[2] The closest any of them ever gets to perception is "I *felt* my language change." When pressured by the minister who wants an impressive testimony about the manifestation in front of the congregation, some (as Nohoč Felipe, Chapter 3) will hesitate and say that maybe they did speak in tongues, they are not sure, and so on.

Lorenzo asks if anybody felt anything, and Floriano comes to the front, facing the congregation. He says that he did feel something, and he thinks that maybe he also had a change of language, but he doesn't know. [And this after about fifteen minutes of tremendous vocalization!] Lorenzo, who had been passing from one supplicant to the other during the prayer for the Holy Spirit, confirms that indeed Floriano has spoken in tongues. So has his wife Francisca. She herself is not sure; she says she felt joy, but she does not know for sure if her language changed.

2 This would rule out "feedback," which means that the speaker hears his own performance, an important mechanism for control, correction, and probably thus memory in speech behavior.

Yet, during the next dissociative episode, the subject has no trouble repeating the utterance in the very same form once more (in Juan D. L.'s case, for instance, within the same period of three months). The impression thus arises that memory skips the waking state, operating from trance episode to trance episode. What is learned in dissociation is remembered only in that state. In other words, if we imagined the various mental states as a series of horizontally arranged layers, we could say that memory does not seem to function vertically from state to state, but horizontally, within one and the same state. It could be argued that, rather than a state-bound functioning of the memory, we are confronted simply by a permission for certain contents to appear within a certain situation. But it seems to me to be more reasonable to assume that certain contents are bound to the state in which they were learned, in view of a study undertaken at the Department of Psychiatry of the Washington University School of Medicine about learning under the effect of alcohol. Male volunteers performed memory tasks either while sober or while intoxicated. Twenty-four hours later they were tested under the same or different conditions. In tasks measuring recall and interference, learning transfer was better when the subject was intoxicated during both sessions than when he was under the effect of alcohol only during the learning session (Goodwin et al. 1969).

No experimental results are as yet available from investigations of the evolution over time of the memory content acquired in alcohol intoxication. I would propose that memory in other than the conscious state differs qualitatively from the latter. At least this is the impression gained from glossolalists. The imprint produced during hyperarousal dissociation is not very stable and after a while—apparently with individual differences—the system begins to disintegrate. This is the case perhaps because from the very start it was in precarious balance. The utterance structure begins to fade and is progressively blotted out until only vestiges of it remain. Apparently with the application of considerable volitional effort, some ministers manage to salvage these vestiges and incorporate them into their devotional performance. But even for them the channel directed toward external stimuli, so impermeable to all but the most specific commands at the outset, loses its selectivity. Thus, for instance, toward the end of the summer of 1970, Lorenzo forbade me to use the floodlamp I carried to take color motion pictures in the church. "It does something to my prayer, I don't know what," he said.

Generally, within the congregation, the fading of the ability to achieve glossolalia is attributed to sinning (see Trinidad's account). On the subjective level, the attenuation may lead to loss of interest in the behavior. *Hermano* Goyito, for instance, of the Mérida congregation, one of the earliest converts of Oscar Gill, has drifted away, in attitude if not in formal membership, and is now more interested in Baha'í. Or it may result in anxiety, and in that case substitute behavior will be sought out, as Emilio did in the spring of 1970, or the subjects will push themselves into experiences resulting in visions, as happened with Anselmo and Peregrino of the Yucatecan congregations.

LINGUISTIC ANALYSIS

The strongest argument for the dissociation-based character of the glossolalia utterance is its cross-culturally encountered configuration of patterns. I shall discuss this configuration in two sections: 1) analyzing a sample of those utterances that led to the initial hypothesis, mentioned in the first chapter, and 2) discussing a number of those encountered during fieldwork.

In contrast to the few linguistic analyses extant at the time the present investigation was started (Wolfram 1966; Samarin 1968), I felt, as indicated before, that it was important to consider not simply the vowel-consonant structure of the glossolalia samples but that attention must be devoted to the totality of a given utterance. Some perfectly pedestrian statements about ordinary language will clarify what I understand to be the totality of an utterance. This brief discussion, naturally, focuses only on those aspects relevant in the present context.

An utterance, in running speech, is first of all an audio signal. This signal consists of vowels and consonants, and these alternate according to the phonological rules of the language involved. Neither in English nor in Spanish can the *bd* cluster, for example, stand in initial position, while either *st* or *sl* can assume that position in English but not in Spanish. In both languages a vowel can stand in initial position and it may be followed by another vowel, a consonant, or a consonant cluster.

The vowels and consonants are grouped into units called segmental morphemes (e.g., *John* or *number*), and in our Indo-European language family these are of differing lengths. Segmental morphemes carry an accentual system. In English and Spanish, this is a system of stress, but the rules for placing the stress are different for the two languages. In both languages, however, relative loudness (Hockett 1958:47; Lehiste and Peterson 1959) and length (Fry: 1955) are used to indicate primary and secondary stress levels. In addition, spoken language is characterized by a stress-timed rhythm, i.e., there is a tendency to keep the interval about equal from one primary-stressed syllable to the next. Hockett (1958:53) points this out for English, but similar tendencies also prevail in other languages. Morphemes or their combinations are separated by pauses, but the occurrence of the pauses and the primary stress do not coincide either in English or in Spanish, since in both languages the primary stress can fall on any syllable.

Morphemes are grouped into phrases (sentences) that are of unequal length. Superimposed upon these is a suprasegmental morpheme called intonation, determining in part the meaning. In the English sentence *I am going home* the intonational peak could fall on any one of the four constituents, depending on the communicative intent of the speaker. Every language has a basic set of speech melodies (intonations); the English declarative sentence has a different melody than the Spanish or Maya one.

In addition to the audio signal, two properties of ordinary language are of importance in our context. First of all, language is productive (creative). Disregarding such forms as clichés, no sentence uttered is likely to have been uttered in exactly that way before. "Most of our linguistic experience," Chomsky says, "is with new sentences; once we have mastered a language, the class of sentences with which we can operate fluently and without difficulty or hesitation is so vast that we can regard it as infinite" (1964:50). And second, speech serves for communication. The speech act transmits a specific message from the speaker to the hearer and presupposes that both partners possess the same linguistic code. Speech as communicative behavior requires consciousness, i.e., the speaker needs to be in perceptive and interpretive contact with the environment, aware of himself, his memory functions operative.

No cumulative body of data is available to us in the literature when we attempt to discover in what way a glossolalia utterance is like or unlike an ordinary-language utterance as outlined above. Few glossolalia utterances have been transcribed, and those that have been published—and this is a crucial point—are incompletely recorded. Stress indication is often omitted, and not one of the transcriptions I have had occasion to examine gives the intonation pattern. The latter omission is understandable. As Hockett points out,

> Until recently, intonation was more or less tacitly
> ignored by most linguistic scholars on the assumption
> that it did not vary significantly from language to
> language, or that anything so "natural" warranted
> serious consideration. . . . Recent research suggests
> that every language has a system of basic speech
> melodies which is as unique to the language as its set
> of vowels and consonant phonemes [1958:34].

And so Samarin says (1968:74), "Some syllables [in glossolalia] get extra stress which is also accompanied by greater volume. The incidence of this stress is probably to be ex-

plained by intonational and emotional factors, not linguistic ones in the strictest sense." And thus, considering
intonation not a linguistic factor, he failed to record it. In
the same vein, Jaquith states (1967:8), "The transcriptions
have been marked for segmental phonemes, syllable boundaries and contour-final junctures. Features such as stress,
vowel length and intonation have been left unmarked to
simplify the orthography."

In other words, the literature contains truncated utterances that, to my mind, are only of limited usefulness for
a thoroughgoing analysis. No truly meaningful statement
can be made with part of the data missing.

For the transcription, I first wrote down the phonetic
pattern. This is not easy since the delivery is usually fast,
the utterances, or rather their sections, brief, and there is
no cue such as vocabulary or sentence structure against
which to check the transcription. Except in the case of the
Streams of Power performance, there is a confusing jumble
of many different simultaneous utterances from which the
ear of the transcriber has to pick out the line of the particular
sample, as the ear of the conductor would the melody line
of a single instrument in an orchestral presentation. (Except
for such tracks as [ʔu ʔu ʔu], the individual vocal coloring
is preserved.) This takes a great deal of practice. Allowing
the transcription to get "cold" and then listening to the
tape again while reading along with the written record helps
to improve the rendition of such details as the number of
similar pulses in a bar or whether there is a unaspirated
[t] or rather a [d]. The pauses, stresses, intonation (and, in
the Mexican samples, also volume and intensity) are so
readily discernible that not much subsequent correction was
required. Following up a suggestion by Professor James E.
Dittes,[3] I had three graduate students in anthropology
individually transcribe one of the Streams of Power utterances. I gave only minimal instructions such as the symbols
to be used for the various features and the sequence in

[3] Editor of the *Journal for the Scientific Study of Religion*.

which it was most convenient to carry out the transcription. In the course of one hour, working with a 7–1/2 sec. utterance, each one was able to sketch out the pattern. Predictably, since none of them had any phonetics training, they did not hear the glottal stops, and one of them had trouble distinguishing the primary and secondary stress. But they had no difficulty perceiving the intonation pattern, especially the peak ("like a question," one of them said) and the final drop ("as if a record player is shut off and the needle is left on the record").

As to the form of the transcription, I evolved only one unconventional notational device, because I found it more instructive than the conventional digits, for the intonation pattern: it is given separately from the phonetic signal, showing its pitch with respect to an individual middle range (represented by a center line) in the shape of a wave.

The vowels have the following pronunciation: a as in father; i as in thick; ɯ as in Rumanian *romîn;* ɛ as in dapple; ø as in German *Öl;* o as in Spanish *nombre;* u as in foot; ɔ as in maul; and ə as in *a*ccount. The stops are all unaspirated; the s in the Spanish samples is not a speech sound but is produced with the teeth almost touching and the tongue curled tightly behind the lower teeth, resulting in a tense hiss; ʔ is the glottal stop. The primary stress is represented by '', the secondary by '; the symbol : after a vowel indicates length.

In discussing the data, I am calling the smallest unit, usually a consonant+vowel, or rarely a consonant+vowel +consonant group, a pulse. Pulses are united into bars, which are separated from each other by a pause. This pause is usually about as long as that between two words in English. Several bars form a phrase. The pause between them is approximately as long as that between two successive English sentences in running speech. An utterance consists of several phrases, an episode of several utterances.

It is interesting to note here that while the phonetic inventory of the recorded glossolalia utterances cannot conveniently be arranged by distinctive feature (e.g., they are not all "grave" in terms of the distinctive feature theory, that is, pronounced at the periphery of the oral cavity), an arrangement of the phones by effort, that is, by energy expended in articulation, provides a key to the glossolalia utterance by indicating which pulse requires a high energy level and which a medium or low one. The data used for this aspect of the anaylsis are summarized in Table 2.

TABLE 2

PHONETIC INVENTORY OF SAINT VINCENT GLOSSOLALIA BY EFFORT*

Consonants			Vowels			
Occlusion effort			Intensity			
high	medium	low	high	high mid	low mid	low
stops:	liquid:	nasal:	i	o	ε	a
ʔ	l	n	u		ɔ	
k g	nasal:				ə	
t d	m					
p						
glides (fortis):						
y						
h						

* Energy output needed to utter the respective sound.

THE TAPES

Preliminary remarks. The transcriptions from the tapes given in the same order in which the respective congregations were discussed, are represented in two sections: intonation on the left, vocalization on the right. Intonation is *perceived* intonation, represented by such factors as loudness, intensity, pitch, or occasionally "crowding," the occurrence in a bar of several more pulses than before. That the pattern perceived by the transcriber has physical reality is demonstrated by the sound spectrogram shown in Figure 7 (p. 109), presenting similar peaks and decays as the other, more protracted utterances transcribed without mechanical aid. Vocalization is the inventory of sounds uttered by the speaker.

Project Tapes
The five samples transcribed from the Streams of Power tape illustrate the following points:

Figure 2. This is a perfect unit utterance with an onset in the middle range, a single peak at the beginning of phrase 2, and a decay to the lowest pitch level at the end of phrase 4. The peak coincides with [u], higher and thus involving more effort than the [o] in the same position in the other phrases.

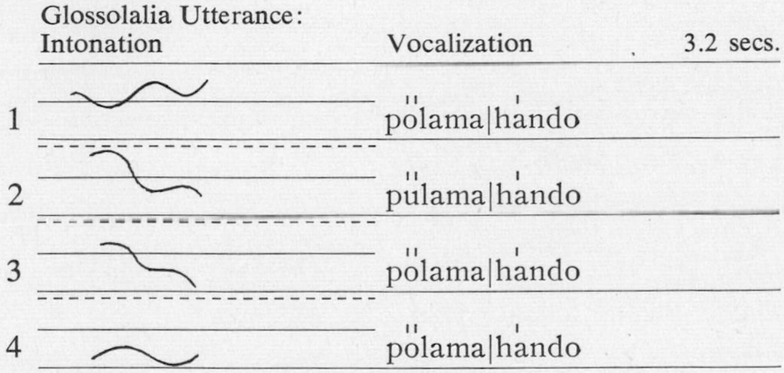

Glossolalia Utterance:

Intonation	Vocalization	3.2 secs.

Fig. 2. Saint Vincent Glossolalia: Man.

Figure 3. This utterance is somewhat longer, and the peak does not occur until the end of phrase 3, from where it carried over into the first bar of phrase 4. The peak is anticipated by a phenomenon I call "crowding," with five pulses occupying the bar instead of one or two as before. The rise on the [i]: at the end of phrase 3 is remarkable here: if an [i] in running discourse is to be as loud as the other vowels surrounding it, increased energy output is needed, i.e., an additional effort. A change from [a] to [i] thus already involves an increase in energy with respect to the [a] of the preceding pulse, and then there is another effort evident, seen in the rise of the pitch. Further examination of the figure shows that, instead of a decay, a slight recovery occurs (something like the second wind of a runner) at the end of phrase 5 going over into phrase 6, and by that time, it seems, the energy level is so depleted that the decay is truly precipitous, and the last bar of phrase 6 is hardly audible. The utterance also has a phonological rule: *nt* follows only *u* and *o*, *nd* only *a*.

Glossolalia Utterance:
Intonation   Vocalization   10.5 secs.

1 húntala|hún

2 maʔtan|diɛ

3 húntala|hanandada di:

4 kóntola|handala

5 húntala|handala|handí

6 kúntala|handí: [honto]

Fig. 3. Saint Vincent Glossolalia: Woman.

Figure 4. All the bars begin with the high-energy stops; in bars 3 and 4 and *d* after the *n* is not the start for a new pulse but acts as an intrusive stop (glide consonant) after the *n;* the peak occurs on the first pulse of the second bar in phrase 4 of six phrases. Note here the occurrence of one of the two pulses of the utterance ending in the constriction of the glottal stop simultaneously with the peak, as an indication of the greater tightening of the throat muscles at this point in the trance event. The other one also coincides with an elevation in phrase 2.

Figure 5. In the service of Adoration, as pointed out above, glossolalia usually occurs singly, i.e., in an orderly fashion, with one speaker waiting out the utterance and

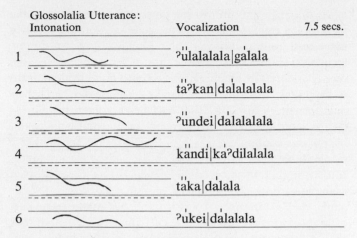

Fig. 4. Saint Vincent Glossolalia: Man.

interpretation of the other. At one spot on the tape, however, there is an overlap of several utterances, all involving
the pulse "ya ?." The sample given in this figure comes from
that section. It begins on a pitch higher than that heard in
the other utterances. The pulse frequency is very high, the
phone and pulse inventory extremely restricted. The peak
comes with a tremendous burst of pulse frequency leading
to it in the first bar of phrase 3, then being accomplished in
the second bar of that phrase, pushing the pitch an octave
and a half above the level of the first pulse of that phrase,
and with this enormous effort exhausting all available
energy, there comes a steep drop ending in a sigh.

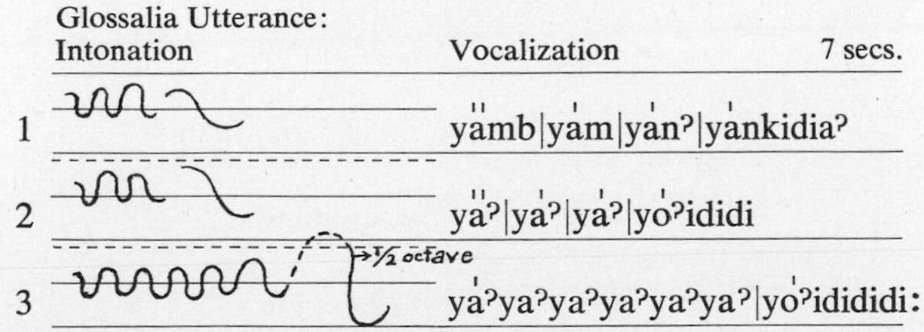

Glossalia Utterance:
Intonation   Vocalization   7 secs.

1   yámb|yám|yán?|yankidia?

2   ya̋?|ya'|ya'?|yo?ididi

→½ octave

3   ya?ya?ya?ya?ya?ya?|yo?ididídi:

Fig. 5. Saint Vincent Glossolalia: Woman.

Figure 6. In addition to the glossolalia utterances by the members of the Streams of Power congregation, the Henney tapes also contain one by their Dutch evangelist. If one compares his utterance with those of his parishioners, the model orientation of the latter becomes quite evident. Two of his pulses, "hunda" and "handa," keep recurring in their pulse inventory also. In other features, however, his glossolalia is quite different. His bars are of unequal length, and his phrases contain from two to four bars. He has neither a recognizable peak nor a decay at the end of his utterance. Rather, it concludes on a slight rise. Figure 6 is, thus, an example of how the evangelist has salvaged sections, remnants, of his utterance structure and has made them part of his performance. Juan L. A., a minister in Yucatán, has been able to stabilize a very similar pattern. He was converted by the Mexican evangelist Oscar Gill in 1959, and in 1970 he still had available a glossolalia utterance of con-

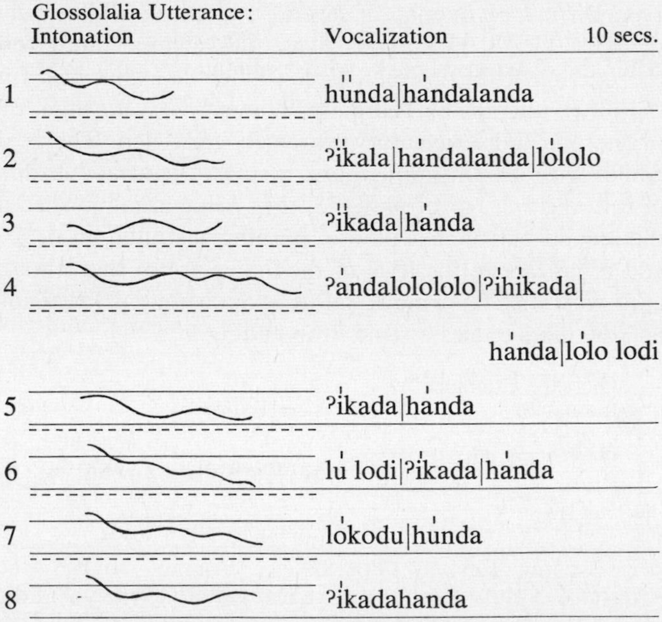

Glossolalia Utterance:

Intonation	Vocalization	10 secs.
1	hünda|händalanda	
2	ʔïkala|händalanda|lololo	
3	ʔïkada|hända	
4	ʔändalolololo|ʔihïkada|	
	hända|lólo lodi	
5	ʔikada|hända	
6	lu lodi|ʔïkada|hända	
7	lókodu|hünda	
8	ʔïkadahanda	

Fig. 6. Saint Vincent Glossolalia: Dutch Evangelist.

siderable length. It is accompanied by some kinetic manifestations, especially when he kneels, and the behavior does, on occasion, "run away" with him, escalating the slight dissociation present into a true discharge. Quite likely, the Dutch evangelist of the Saint Vincent Streams of Power congregation would display a similar behavior, were he observed over an extended period with these points in mind.

Figure 7. Comes from the tent revival tape. It is a sound spectrogram of the only glossolalia utterance clearly audible above the very high noise level of the tape. It starts at a high pitch and with a pulse frequency rate so elevated that the phonetic pattern is obliterated, giving the impression of a rhythmically pulsing scream. We see a succession of peaks, roughly fourteen of them, and a very clear sloping of the overall curve, indicating a gradual drop in energy level. After the tenth peak, we can hear a few articulated pulses: *palomalalaya*, strikingly similar to the phrases heard on the Saint Vincent tapes, and again after the eleventh peak: *kalomahala*. The drop occurs, very steeply, after the fourteenth peak, with a glissando "ah" ending in a sigh and a barely audible "Jesus." There is no interpretation. The fact that the articulated bars suddenly appear late in the total utterance seems to demonstrate that a drop in energy level was needed for articulation to become possible or, stating it differently, there seems to be an energy level beyond which articulation no longer occurs.

The utterance selected for Figure 8, from a main-line church in the Houston, Texas, area, contains intelligible

55 s

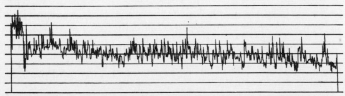

Fig. 7. Tent Revival Glossolalia: Woman. Sound spectrogram; 3 mm/sec., paper calibrated to horizontal steps of 5 decibels (prepared by Phonetics Laboratory, The Ohio State University, Columbus, Ohio).

words and no pulses devoid of semantic content. Yet it is my judgment that this also is glossolalia rather than an ordinary-language utterance because of the following features. It starts off at a relatively high pitch, almost as high as the tent revival utterance. The pulse-frequency rate is considerably elevated, "panting" or "urgent" to use the expressions of some authors who describe glossolalia. But principally its stress and intonation pattern is the same as that shown in Figures 2–5: we have the regular organization into bars and phrases of equal length, and twice, the bar boundary cuts across the semantic level, once in phrase 1, separating prais/ing, and in phrase 3 where the bar pause cuts a vowel in half, making *says* into [sɛ?ɛz]. The peak, since the pitch is already so very high, cannot easily go in that direction; it finds expression in a greater frequency of the pulses, and, as in Figure 3, recovery is attempted, once in phrase 3 and again in phrase 4. The decay of the utterance sets in with *real* in (5).

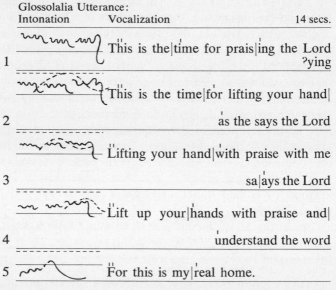

Glossolalia Utterance:
Intonation   Vocalization   14 secs.

1   This is the|time for prais|ing the Lord
                                          ?ying

2   This is the time|for lifting your hand|
                            as the says the Lord

3   Lifting your hand|with praise with me
                            sa|ays the Lord

4   Lift up your|hands with praise and|
                      understand the word

5   For this is my|real home.

Fig. 8. National Educational Television Network: Woman. Peaks of intonation are indicated by dotted lines.

The Umbanda tapes contain an incidence of violent "possession" that occurred at a private session of the cult. This happened to a man who occasionally had problems with an "unruly spirit." We do not hear any glossolalia, but simply a breathing pattern (Fig. 9), showing the same curve as seen in the glossolalia utterance: a medium-level onset, a tense, high-frequency (more and more rapid breathing) peak culminating in a little shriek, and then a rather brief drop with a grunted sigh.

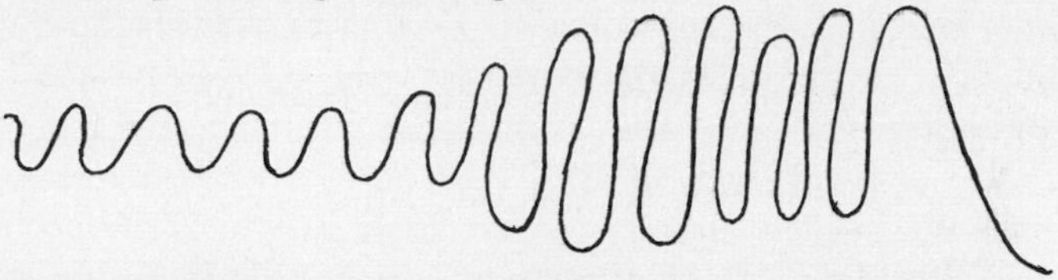

Fig. 9. Umbanda Cult: Man Breathing in Trance. Breathing perceived as an audio signal by the transcriber.

At the same session, a woman was said to be possessed by an *orixá* spirit called Iemanjá (Fig. 10). We hear her rather labored breathing, then three bars of a melody from another woman present, then once more her breathing. She then goes into vocalization again, with a very high, flutelike, unarticulated motif duplicating the second bar of the above melody. At intervals, she produces three different variations of the same bar. The first variation on the melody motif starts one and a half octaves above the onset of the original bar. This is followed by very rapid hyperventilation and a vocalization without articulation, representable in an intonation curve. It rises an octave over the base tone, breaks, rises another half octave,[4] and then drops steeply into laughter: it is said that a child spirit has arrived and is possessing her.

In addition to providing us with an inarticulate dissociative vocalization exhibiting the same intonation curve as the glossolalia utterance, the woman's singing in the altered

[4] The recurrence of the one-and-a-half octave step (see Fig. 5) is intriguing and makes one wonder about the neurophysiological mechanisms involved.

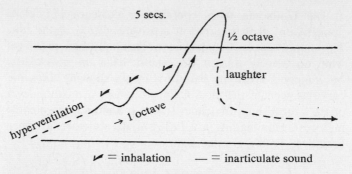

Fig. 10. Umbanda Cult: Woman's Inarticulate Trance
Phrase.

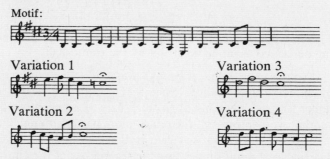

Fig. 11. Umbanda Cult: Singing Variations of a Motif in
Trance.

state (Fig. 11) gives us an instructive demonstration of the
alteration that the memory function undergoes as the subject passes from light to deeper dissociation: with each
successive variation, the original motif becomes more and
more obliterated.

Tapes Recorded in the Field
Mexico City. Figures 12–15 are examples of utterances occurring in the Cuarta Iglesia. The phone and pulse inventory
varies little from speaker to speaker (see Fig. 11, where
some of the utterances of the congregation are given as
background to Juan's). This correlates with the fact that

Pastor Torres has been with the congregation for some seven years, so that it may be assumed that he has guided the majority of the members into the glossolalia behavior. They would thus reflect his inventory, which, unfortunately, I had no chance to record because it was of very low intensity and volume.

New features added to the figures are: a sample of an ordinary language utterance, to demonstrate the intonation of the Spanish sentence as against that of the glossolalia. In singing, Juan has a tenor voice, but in glossolalia his pitch does not go high; instead, there are varying levels of volume and intensity. These are transcribed as forte (f, ff) or piano (p, pp), and as 1–3 respectively; + represents clapping. Pitch, volume, and intensity do not always coincide, thus giving the impression of an upbeat in I. By II, this upbeat effect is lost.

The glossolalia episode, recorded on 16 July, 1968, consists of five utterances (I–V). Again, as seen in the spectrogram from the tent revival (Fig. 7), there is a clear overall sloping energy gradient, with the vowels going from high-effort ones ([i], [ɯ], etc.) to the low-level shwa ([ə]).

I. This consists of six phrases, each a complete curve with medium onset, peak, and decay. In addition, this utterance has an overall peak at phrase 3.

II. The end of I is marked by a brief return to ordinary language, clapping, and then II starts. It has ten phrases, with overall peaks at phrases 2 and 5, followed by crowding in phrase 6. The decay goes lower than in I and, for the first time, *shwa* appears in phrases 9 and 10.

III. This is very brief, only four phrases, again peaking in phrase 2. A note needs to be added here about the clapping indicated in the transcription (to be discussed under kinetic behavior pp. 132–33). When singing, Juan keeps perfect time, accenting the rhythm of the hymns, as does the rest of the congregation. Sometimes he also claps during prayer in ordinary language. In that case, the clap comes on the accented syllables and occasionally also in a pause:

"Es todo, Señor . . . Señor Jesucristo . . . Espíritu Santo
\+   \+   \+   \+   \+   \+   \+
. . ." As energy levels wane, Juan also adds clapping while
still dissociated, but in that case there is no attempt to keep
time. A syncopating effect sometimes arises, but it seems
purely accidental. It is as if two brain structures were operating simultaneously without central command. (This phenomenon will be discussed in greater detail in chap. 5.)

IV. He coughs, there is a hardly audible bar, then a
steep rise into high volume and intensity. The [k] of phrase
5 is so strongly occluded as to give the effect of choking.

There follows some unstructured articulation, very indistinct, interspersed with words and fragmented bars, in
what seems a struggle about which way to go—into waking
or into a recovery of the dissociation level. Bars 6–20 (not
shown) reflect this teetering between two states on the substratum of a dropping energy level. The clenched [s] gives
way to [d], more and more *shwas* appear, until in phrase 19
we have

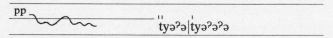

Then comes a pause, a slight rise, and a complete decay with

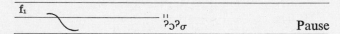

Finally, V is even more prolonged. In its twenty-four
phrases there is a ff$_2$ peak in phrase 2 with [ʔɯ ʔia|tyəʔɛh],
a secondary one comes in phrase 11, but the level is irretriev-
able, and the end comes in phrase 24 with

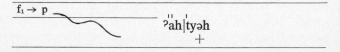

There is a pause, then a return to ordinary language with
"*Aleluia, gloria ti*," and so on. The whole, truly dramatic
episode lasts 3 minutes and 44 seconds.

Glossolalia Utterance (f, p = volume; 1-3 = tenseness; + = clapping):

Intonation	Vocalization	9 secs.

I.

1 f_2 $ʔ\overset{\shortmid\shortmid}{a}ʔa|s^iøh$

2 f_2 $ʔ\overset{\shortmid\shortmid}{a}wa|s^iøh$

3 ff_3 $ʔ\overset{\shortmid\shortmid}{u}wa|s^iøh$ Pause

4 f_2 $ʔ\overset{\shortmid\shortmid}{a}hɯʔ|s^iøh$ Pause

5 f_2 $ʔ\overset{\shortmid\shortmid}{a}hi|s^iøh$ Longer Pause

6 $f_1 \to p$ $ʔ\overset{\shortmid\shortmid}{a}hə|syøh$

Pause . . . Speaking . . . + + → Glossolalia

		23 secs.

II.

1 ff_2 $s^i\overset{\shortmid\shortmid}{ø}h|s^iøh$

2 ff_3 $s\overset{\shortmid\shortmid}{i}høh|s^iøh$

3 ff_3 $s\overset{\shortmid\shortmid}{i}høh|s^iøh$

4 ff_2 $ʔ\overset{\shortmid\shortmid}{ə}h|sihøh$

5 ff_3 $ʔ\overset{\shortmid\shortmid}{ɯ}hsiah|s^iøh$

6 f_3 $ʔ\overset{\shortmid\shortmid}{ɯ}buliaʔɯ|s^iahs^iøh$

7 f_3 ff_3 $ʔ\overset{\shortmid\shortmid}{ɯ}:h|s^iøh$

8 f_2 $p \to pp$ $ʔ\overset{\shortmid\shortmid}{a}h|s^iyøh$

9 p_1 $ʔ\overset{\shortmid\shortmid}{a}i|s^i\overset{\shortmid}{ə} s^iə$ Coughing . . . + + +

10 p $ʔ\overset{\shortmid\shortmid}{a}i|s^iə$ Background, woman: siə, siə

ɯ = as î in "Român"

Speaking . . . + + → Glossolalia

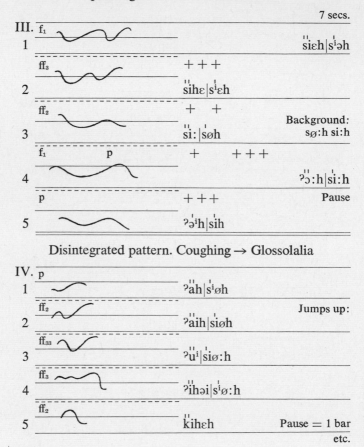

Disintegrated pattern. Coughing → Glossolalia

Fig. 12. Cuarta Iglesia: Glossolalia of Juan D. L., 16
July 1968. Declarative sentence: "Gloria al Señor Jesus
Cristo."

Figure 13 represents Juan's utterance, the first of an
episode, almost exactly a year later. The pulse inventory
has not changed, but it is longer than the initial utterance
of the previous year and both volume and intensity have
dropped.

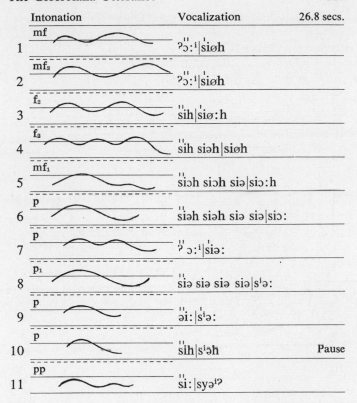

| Intonation | Vocalization | 26.8 secs. |

1 mf ʔɔ̈:ⁱ|si̇øh

2 mf₂ ʔɔ̈:ⁱ|si̇øh

3 f₂ s̈ih|si̇ø:h

4 f₃ s̈ih si̇əh|si̇øh

5 mf₁ s̈iɔh si̇ɔh hci̇s|si̇ɔ:h

6 p s̈iəh si̇əh si̇ə si̇ə|si̇ɔ:

7 p ʔ̈ ɔ:ⁱ|si̇ə:

8 p₁ s̈iə si̇ə si̇ə si̇ə|sⁱə:

9 p ə̈i:|sⁱə:

10 p s̈ih|sⁱəh   Pause

11 pp s̈i:|syəⁱʔ

Fig. 13. Cuarta Iglesia: Glossolalia of Juan D. L., 17 June 1969.

Figure 14 is an utterance by Juan, once more the initial one of an episode, two months later. The struggle to achieve vocalization seems very arduous. Juan claps extremely fast, then slows down, speeds up once more, prays loudly, but no glossolalia ensues. Finally, there is a single phrase, [ʔai siɔ siø:], but the attempt aborts. His prayer becomes long-drawn-out and is at variance with his fast clapping (something that Marks [1969] calls "paradoxical command"). Finally, the glossolalia level is achieved and, perhaps due to the effort expended in reaching it, there is now considerable fluctuation of the intonation with respect to

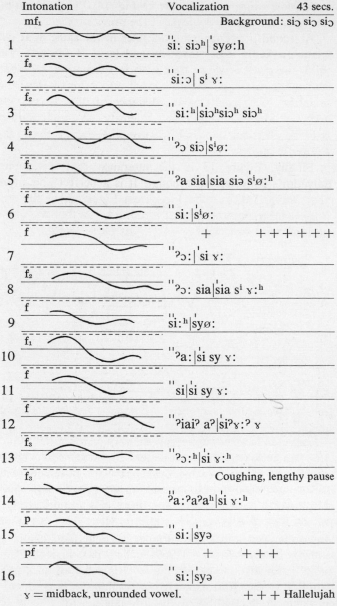

Intonation	Vocalization	43 secs.
mf_1		Background: siɔ siɔ siɔ
1	''si: siɔʰ|'syø:h	
2 f_3	''si:ɔ|'sⁱ ɤ:	
3 f_2	''si:ʰ|siɔʰsiɔʰ siɔʰ	
4 f_2	''ʔɔ siɔ|'sⁱø:	
5 f_1	''ʔa sia|sia siə 'sⁱø:ʰ	
6 f	''si:|'sⁱø:	
7 f	+ +++++	
	''ʔɔ:|'si ɤ:	
8 f_2	''ʔɔ: sia|sia sⁱ ɤ:ʰ	
9 f	''si:ʰ|'syø:	
10 f_1	''ʔa:|'si sy ɤ:	
11 f	''si|si sy ɤ:	
12 f	''ʔiaiʔ aʔ|'siʔɤ:ʔ ɤ	
13 f_3	''ʔɔ:ʰ|'si ɤ:ʰ	
14 f_3	Coughing, lengthy pause	
	''ʔa:ʔaʔaʰ|'si ɤ:ʰ	
15 p	''si:|'syə	
16 pf	+ +++	
	''si:|'syə	

ɤ = midback, unrounded vowel. +++ Hallelujah

Fig. 14. Cuarta Iglesia: Glossolalia of Juan D. L., 26 August 1969.

the middle range (see left side of Fig. 14). Neither volume nor intensity attains the level of the previous year.

A second utterance achieved later in the same altar call has a markedly lower intensity and lasts 31 seconds. The third one gives evidence that Juan is attempting, by whatever mechanism, to "push" himself into a higher-level dissociation. This results in an utterance of only 17 seconds, with considerable volume and intensity, its initial phrases only an overlong [ʔɔː]. With dropping energy level, the key pulse returns.

Finally, Figure 15 is the utterance that interrupted Salvador's conversional account. It is a perfect unit utterance, except for the upbeat in phrase 1 identical to the ones from Saint Vincent in its medium onset, rise to a peak, and rapid decay, but not, of course, in its pulse inventory.

Glossolalia Utterance: Intonation	Vocalization	2.5 secs.
1	kaʔ|siaʔ|sia	
2	ʔiya|ki|siaʔ	
3	si ʔə	Pause

Fig. 15. Cuarta Iglesia: Glossolalia of Salvador A. Z., 1968. Declarative sentence: "Entonces fue mucho gozo hablando → en nuevas lenguas."

Utzpak, Yucatán. Of the individuals represented in Figures 16–19, Lorenzo is the only Spanish speaker. Some members of the congregation maintained that he probably also spoke Maya as his mother tongue but would not admit it because of the loss of prestige this might involve. The others are bilingual Maya and Spanish, with more fluency in the former. Their Spanish has a heavy overlay of Maya phonemes, evidenced especially by the glottalization or lengthening of initial stops. The language in the church is Spanish.

Maya is an American Indian language, a member of the

Macro-Penutian language family. It is a tonal language, that is, high tone versus low tone distinguishes meaning, as does vowel length. Only a consonant can stand in initial position. In contrast to English, vowel length does not coincide with the intonation peak, as shown, for example, in the sentence: $\text{ʔa k'áat}^2 \rightarrow \text{ká šíʔi}^1\text{ken}^1$ (a double vowel is long [Blair and Vermont-Salas 1967]). As in English, the primary intonation peak may fall on any one of several segments within a phrase.

Figure 16 is a key utterance of Lorenzo, recorded in 1969. The rest of his glossolalia episode is still too fast to transcribe properly. It exhibits the standard intonational features.

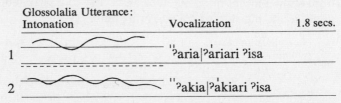

Glossolalia Utterance:

Intonation	Vocalization	1.8 secs.
1	''ʔaria|'ʔariari ʔisa	
2	''ʔakia|ʔ'akiari ʔisa	

Fig. 16. Utzpak, Yucatán: Glossolalia of Lorenzo, 13 July 1969.

Figure 17 is Lorenzo a year later. The key pulse is there, but there are elaborations, the utterance is longer and slow enough for transcription, with a peak in phrase 3.

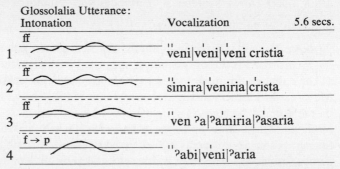

Glossolalia Utterance:

Intonation	Vocalization	5.6 secs.
1 ff	''veni|v'eni|v'eni cristia	
2 ff	''simira|veniria|crista	
3 ff	''ven ʔa|ʔ'amiria|ʔ'asaria	
4 f → p	''ʔabi|veni|ʔaria	

Fig. 17. Utzpak, Yucatán: Glossolalia of Lorenzo, 23 July 1970.

Figure 18, by Emilio, a Maya speaker, is the initial utterance of an episode lasting 13 minutes and 7 seconds. The key pulse is similar but not identical to that of Lorenzo. The episode shows a number of recoveries and ends in a prolonged pattern of [tyə sə sə].

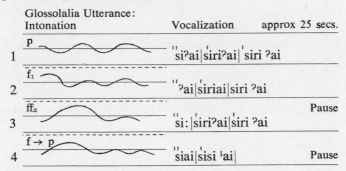

Fig. 18. Utzpak, Yucatán: Glossolalia of Emilio, 13 July 1969.

Figure 19, finally, is a good example of the threshold to stereotypy. Alfredo, a Maya speaker, is a recent glossolalist (starting in June 1970; soundtrack recorded in July). He is still in transition from his own innovations to the key pulse of his guides, very fast. His phrases 8–10, in addition, could not be heard well enough for transcription because they were too low. His own pulses are beginning to make way for the "*siriai*" heard so much in Emilio. Probably Emilio more than Lorenzo was his guide into the behavior.

In summary, we can say that while both the ordinary-language and the glossolalia utterance represent an audio signal, the glossolalia utterance exhibits important agreements across seven cultural settings and with the background of four different languages.

a) On the phonetic level, every pulse begins with a consonant and there are no initial consonant clusters. Nearly always the pulse is open, i.e., it does not end in a consonant.

b) Bars are usually of equal duration, especially if the pauses are also considered, as one would do in music.

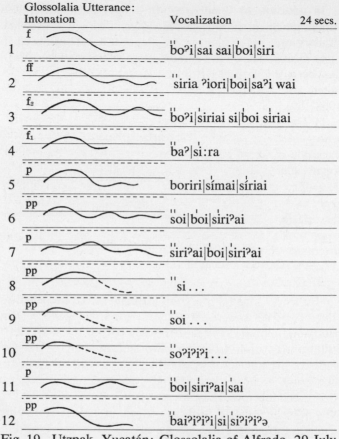

Fig. 19. Utzpak, Yucatán: Glossolalia of Alfredo, 29 July 1970.

   c) The accentual system is one of stress, with a primary and secondary accent. The primary one falls on the first pulse of each bar, giving the impression of scanning, in a trochaic rhythm. The primary stress is always preceded by a pause.

   d) Phrases are of equal length. Within an utterance unit (i.e., with one peak), the intonation pattern regularly shows an onset in the medium range, a peak, and a sloping gradient leading to an often precipitous decay.

In addition to these agreements on the phonetic and suprasegmental level, there are also other cross-cultural similarities:

e) Glossolalia is not productive. Once an audio signal has been internalized, it becomes stereotyped. This was noted also by other observers (Pattison 1968:80; Spoerri 1968:150).

f) The stereotyped utterance mirrors that of the person who guided the glossolalist into the behavior. There is little variation of sound patterns within the group arising around a particular guide.

g) The glossolalia utterance changes over time, apparently as a function of the attenuation of the hyperarousal dissociation. This is perceivable in a loss of intensity (loudness, pitch), increase in pattern variation, lengthening of utterance time,[5] and shortening of the episode (sum of utterances given at one time.)

h) Glossolalia is lexically noncommunicative. The utterer of the glossolalia and his listener do not share a linguistic code. Rather, as Spoerri puts it, "Die Glossolalie schliesst . . . den Verlust der Informations- und Kommunikationsseite der Rede in sich; die Sprache wird zur Lautmusik" (1968:152).[6] What it does communicate is, initially, the commitment to the group and, later on, a sharing of its ritual behavior with all that this involves on the personal and social side.

Discussion

Such agreement of pattern despite linguistic and cultural differences,[7] to my mind, can be explained only if we assume that the glossolalia is not simply uttered while in dissocia-

[5] From 16 July 1968 to 26 August 1969, Juan D. L.'s average individual phrase time increased from 2.3 to 2.5, and then to 2.7 seconds; that of Lorenzo from 13 July 1969 to 23 July 1970 from 0.9 to 1.4 seconds.

[6] Glossolalia involves . . . the privation of the informative and communicative side of discourse; speech becomes musical sound."

[7] We are not here concerned with what speakers believe about glossolalia. The belief systems vary from culture to culture and are the domain of the group's theology.

tion but is an artifact of the mental state, or rather of its neurophysiological processes. It is thought (Gardner 1963: 291), for example, that in epilepsy the cortex is driven by discharges from subcortical structures. I am proposing that something similar is happening during glossolalia. In some manner, the glossolalist switches off cortical control. Then, with considerable effort, at least initially, he establishes a connection between his speech center and some subcortical structure, which then proceeds to drive the former. Thereupon the vocalization behavior becomes an audible manifestation of the rhythmical discharges of this subcortical structure, resulting in the described pattern. The most striking characteristic of this discharge is the fact that it has a variable frequency and amplitude, producing one complete wave from onset over peak to decay in anywhere from perhaps two seconds to six seconds or longer and amplitudes from ordinary speech variations in pitch up to an octave and a half. The latter seems to be something of a physiological constant, showing up, for example, on the Saint Vincent tapes (Fig. 4), in Umbanda (Figs. 9–10), as well as on a commercially available record about a rite of exorcism (Allen), where the medium is apparently also in hyperarousal dissociation, and goes just barely beyond this range.

I want to propose then that glossolalia should be defined as a vocalization pattern, a speech automatism, that is produced on the substratum of hyperarousal dissociation, reflecting directly, in its segmental and suprasegmental structure, neurophysiologic processes present in this mental state. It is not circular, to my mind, to continue by stating that the presence of the patterns identified above marks a speech behavior as glossolalia. Thus, for instance, a tape kindly placed at my disposal by Professor Roger Wescott of the Department of Anthropology at Drew University and containing a lengthy vocalization produced by the subject (Mr. R. of London) while under the effect of LSD-25 is not in this sense glossolalia. The LSD[8] given to Mr. R. doubt-

---

[8] Dosage unknown.

less produced dissociation; he stumbled into vocalization inadvertently and was for more than half an hour unable to control the behavior, so in this way we find agreement with the glossolalia manifestation as we have come to know it. But: the sound track does not have the same patterning as the utterances reported here. The pulses are spoken at a very high rate, but they also have a richness of sound inventory quite distinct from that heard from glossolalists when they first acquire the behavior. There are no regularly spaced bars or phrases, and no intonation such as in the "naturally" induced glossolalia, with its onset, rise, and decay. After hearing and becoming familiar with the glossolalia of the type about which I report, I felt as if this LSD-induced vocalization episode were a foreign language.

Conversely, apparently there are mental patients whose vocal patterns resemble glossolalia in our sense. Of the several vocalizations on a record assembled by Spoerri (1963) of the speech patterns of such patients, the one produced by a female forty-six-year-old chronic schizophrenic patient is in every way a classical utterance.

5 Kinetic Behavior

Having understood something about glossolalia, we can now describe and possibly elucidate another pattern usually present during hyperarousal dissociation and somehow tied to the vocalization. While dissociated, the subjects are rarely ever motionless. There is movement, kinetic behavior, during all phases of this type of mental state. Not all of these manifestations are qualitatively the same, however. By taking glossolalia as the intermediary, i.e., as the pattern that makes the neurophysiological process perceivable to us, we are able to observe that there is motor behavior accompanying the dissociation, motor behavior intensifying it, and motor behavior interrupting it.

Generally speaking, the first of these, i.e., the motor behavior accompanying the trance, is completely rhythmical.

Cilia is on her knees rocking back and forth, her shoulders shaking. Or she has her palms on the floor, and her trunk moves sideways, left, right, left, right.

Gilberto has his hands on his knees, rocking back and forth, uttering glossolalia.

Emilio shakes his head very rapidly, or he bows lightly up and down while praying in tongues.

At the high points, Gregoria stretches out her arms, her hands fluttering very rapidly back and forth.

Peregrino is kneeling, his left hand grabbing his right elbow, and in this position he bows up and down.

Lorenzo, kneeling, places his hands on his knees, then sits

back on his heels and straightens up alternately, quite fast.
Or he simply rocks back and forth in the same position.

During the prayer for the sick, Martín is standing, his arms
extended upward, alternately folding his hands and
rubbing them together.

This kinetic behavior may take place at varying frequency,
from rather slow to incredibly fast and can conveniently be
arranged on a scale, going from micro- to macropattern:
micropattern

—trembling and shaking
—twitching (face, thorax)
—fingers cramping and stretching (not all simultaneously)
—head shaking
—hand manipulation
—throwing trunk from side to side
—jumping: a) while kneeling
          b) from kneeling to standing
          c) while standing: lifting from heel to toe
—rocking, bowing, arm lifting, while standing or kneeling
macropattern

The closer to the microend of the scale, the more the pattern seems neurologically based and thus occurring in all groups. Perhaps the reason for this phenomenon can be seen in what Benedetti says about certain processes on the level of the neurons: "Sie sind nicht psychisch unbewusst, sondern unbewusst, weil sie nicht psychisch sind" (1969: 153).[1] The more kinetic behavior approaches the macroend of the scale, the more it tends to be peculiar to a group, i.e., the more amenable it becomes to cultural (= group) patterning, although it never becomes as model-oriented as the vocalization pattern. There is a striking parallel here between the [ʔu ʔu ʔu ʔu] vocalization and its variants encountered in all personally observed groups and the different pulse inventories represented in the several congregations.

---

1 "They are not psychically unconscious, but unconscious, because they are not psychical."

As far as memory functions are concerned, it may be significant that the kinetic behavior seems never to be perceived directly. Occasionally there are reports of what others did: "one jumps," or "he somersaulted all through the church," but never accounts in the first person. Again on the above scale, the closer to the macroscale, the easier its imprint on the neurons will be extinguished and the more innovations will appear. Although apparently so closely associated with the glossolalia, kinetic behavior does not seem to be wedded into one automatism with the vocalization.

Thus, for instance, observing Juan D. L. in the Cuarta Iglesia once more in 1969, I noted that not only had his glossolalia slowed down somewhat and lost much of its intensity and volume of the previous year, but also he no longer jumped up during the vocalization. In Mérida, Gregoria had lost her hand flutter by the summer of 1970. Here is another, somewhat more detailed observation:

[Recorded in Utzpak, 20 July 1969] In trance, Peregrino either puts his left arm behind his back, his right arm hanging down, and that way he grabs his right elbow with his left hand and keeps bowing up and down, or he presses his hands together in the motion of a prayer, lifts his arms, and bends up and down in this manner.

[Recorded in Chetumal, 20 July 1970] Two men here have the same kinetic pattern as the one Peregrino showed last year when he visited in Utzpak. Peregrino's, however, has changed. Instead of having his left arm behind his back and bending forward and back, he now lifts both arms, and otherwise stays rigid. Then he lets one arm drop, weaving a bit around his own axis. Of the other two men, one is jumping on his knees occasionally, the other one is rocking back and forth. Peregrino now has both arms up again and rubs his hands together, with hands and fingers perfectly straight. This is a common movement among Yucatecan men when their hands are cold or sweating. But Peregrino's palms do not touch. Rocking on one's knees seems highly characteristic of this congregation;

there is a woman in the aisle now doing it. The two men mentioned earlier are now rocking, while on their knees, their trunks parallel to the ground. A boy in the other aisle does it too, but also rubs his hands together in the manner in which Peregrino does it.

The kinetic behavior seems to share with the vocalization behavior in the same energy pool, and is subject to a concomitant long-term attenuation. Thus in the ministers, who by volition seem to be able to establish a more stable automatism than the laity, the energy content of the kinetic behavior and the glossolalia drop simultaneously; in Lorenzo, for example, evidenced by longer phrases, less frequent utterances, and a larger number of phrases within the utterances in 1970 than in 1969, and on the kinetic level, again by less frequent manifestation and briefer duration.

How closely allied with respect to energy resource the two behavior aspects, vocalization and kinetics, must actually be is evidenced by the following observation:

[23 July 1970] Martín is kneeling before the altar. He seems to have difficulty entering into glossolalia. Up to now he has only achieved the trance step.

During the prayer for the sick [at the conclusion of the same service] Martín is standing, his arms extended upward, alternately folding his hands and rubbing them very lightly together, in a graceful, balletlike, weaving pattern.

[26 July] Martín finally achieves glossolalia, and at that moment, his kinetic pattern becomes very simple, as if all energy were absorbed by this one important step. He just keeps rocking with upstretched arms.

As we leave, I see Martín praying over a sick child. His newly acquired glossolalia is very clear, his kinetic pattern still simplified. He has one hand on the child's head, the other [left] is lifted high, fingers are not moving. His glossolalia is a very rapid, strictly rhythmical stutter.

[28 July] Martín's utterance is still very fast. He cannot pick up the bell signal, and continues with his glossolalia considerably beyond it.

[30 July] Over on the men's side, there is a scene developing
between Martín and some of the other men. Martín's
arms are high with his characteristic weaving pattern.
He is in his very fast, staccato utterance, facing Nacho
and Vicente. Anselmo leans over to him as if trying to
understand.

In other words, at the crucial moment of breaking into
vocalization all energy is drained to achieve this extremely
difficult step. Vocalization continues to be highly strenuous
for a brief while; then, as stereotypy is more securely
established, less energy is absorbed, and the surplus can
once more be employed, as in Martín's case, for the previously acquired kinetic behavior.

A dramatic struggle against attenuation over time and,
to my mind, the anxiety engendered by the perception of
this "slipping away" of the experience, evidenced in both
the vocalization and the kinetic behavior is seen in Emilio's
case. It also reflects the complexity of interaction between
motor behavior and energy resources. Emilio, as will be
recalled, had achieved glossolalia for the first time in De-
cember 1968, and in the summer of 1969 he was still very
much in possession of the behavior. Never exhibiting very
intense kinetics, his utterances are often very long:

[28 June 1969] Emilio, a man with a curious "mouthing"
manner of speaking, bends his trunk lightly up and down
during prayer, while on his knees.

[29 June] Emilio once more goes into glossolalia. He does
not react to Lorenzo's bell, which signals the end of the
prayer. A *corito* is called, and then finally, at the third
stanza, he comes out of his trance.

[6 July] Emilio rocks a little back and forth.

[13 July] During the altar call, Emilio goes into glossolalia.
He does not react to the bell but continues during the
subsequent hymn and *corito*. He goes on during the
testimonies and then into the next altar call. Finally he
goes into a shwa pattern, tsə, tsə, tsə, and ends with
"O Dios mio." But he stays at the altar. During Bible

reading, he is still there, trying to control the volume of
his glossolalia, but apparently not succeeding. Usually
he does not move much during trance, but now he is
shaking, his body moves lightly up and down in a regular
rhythm. At this point his glossolalia is hardly audible.
He stops moving, and simultaneously the glossolalia
becomes louder again.

[2 July 1970] Emilio, a very active glossolalist last year,
is an outstanding participant in the subsequent prayer
for the sick. [Lorenzo tells me later that Emilio has received
the gift of the Holy Spirit of faith healing, of curing by
prayer. The way it manifests itself in Emilio, he says, is that
Emilio feels a powerful urge to do this.] He has acquired
a great deal of impressive kinetic behavior, completely
absent last year. This includes especially a very rapid
back-and-forth movement of the hands parallel to the
ground, and equally rapid head shaking. Occasionally the
impression arises that he is desperately trying to break
into vocalization, i.e., glossolalia, gasping for breath,
doubling up, pressing his arms against his middle. His
glossolalia is occasionally mixed with sections of meaningful
phrases. It is a very long utterance, and at the end of it
Emilio breathes heavily, sits down, pulls out a handkerchief,
and wipes his forehead.

[3 July] Emilio repeats his remarkable kinetic performance,
with the same inventory of movements. Kneeling, he
stretches his hand toward those kneeling before him,
it cramps, then his fingers stretch out, his arm shaking.
He keeps losing his glossolalia, lapsing into seemingly
agonizing attempts to regain it. Occasionally, the utterance
is interspersed with "*obra, obra*" [work your miracle, Lord].
Finally he places both hands on his knees. Some three-
year-olds observe him intently. He swallows several times,
finally gets out his handkerchief to wipe his face.

[4 July] At the prayer for the sick, Emilio once more goes
into a very intense trance and struggle for glossolalia
with almost the same pattern as the night before, except
that at one point, apparently in very considerable
dissociation, he adds a hand flutter, very loose in the wrists.

Then, nearly a month later, after the level of intensity of religious experience had been steadily mounting, there is the entry:

[30 July] Emilio is in glossolalia, with an utterance very much like the one he had last year except shorter, and, as was the case then, he is practically motionless while dissociated.

In other words, during his first summer of glossolalia, Emilio's dissociation is centered on the vocalization. The accompanying kinetic behavior is minimal. The speaking in tongues accords him, as he himself testifies, an all-important dissolution of anxiety. There is thus a decisive psychological drive to keep the vocalization at a level where it will provide the intensity of the discharge he feels he needs. With the inescapability of physiological processes, however, the experience begins to fade. Emilio tries, I think, to regain its former levels by self-manipulation: in low-level dissociation, he presses his arms against his chest to produce the sensation of pressure on the rib cage characteristic of his former, more intense, altered state. He tries to impel himself by richer and richer kinetic patterns. All the while, his glossolalia slips away from him, apparently because, with all this strategy, he depletes his resources even more. The entire process is reminiscent of the desperation of the drug user who takes increasingly larger doses and then switches to a "harder" drug to produce the same high. The events of the summer finally help him to accomplish what he alone could not achieve, i.e., recreate something of the previous intensity of the experience. It is to be expected that his respite will be a temporary one.

As to the motor behavior that seems either to intensify the level of dissociation or to interrupt the glossolalia utterance, it is arhythmical. To my mind this might be interpreted as indicating a control mechanism, brought into play by cortical structures as they attempt to reassert themselves.

In Figure 12 (p. 115), a lengthy glossolalia by Juan D. L., the + marks stand for clapping (each + for one clap). They illustrate the arhythmical quality of this behavior, and, as mentioned, they occur in the total configuration at a spot where the energy level is waning. The autosignal here apparently is capable of whipping up some reinforcement. Such patterns, by the way, are extremely difficult to transcribe. I recall feeling all my own musical and ornamental expectations violated, and I checked and rechecked the rendition, somehow hoping that perhaps I was wrong, that actually the clapping was punctuating the rhythm rather than running erratically contrary to it, as, in fact, it did.

Lorenzo also uses this seemingly erratic clapping to induce or intensify his hyperarousal, as do other members of the Utzpak congregation. There may be other arhythmical motions serving the same purpose, of course, but they are hard to identify, for on occasion it may be impossible to sort the accidental from the control mechanism. The following may be such a case:

During this prayer I note Peregrino's oldest daughter. She is sixteen years old and has been speaking in tongues since August 1969 [this is recorded 20 July, 1970]. She is standing in her seat and quickly goes into an intense glossolalia; her whole body twitches, and occasionally with her left hand she lightly touches her pubic region. The impression arises as if simultaneously there were also an intensification of her trance because of an increase in the loudness of her vocalization.

In addition to arhythmical autosignals, the supplicants are also subjected to arhythmical manipulation, which again serves apparently to induce and on occasion to intensify the dissociation: both the headshaking and the brief jarring of the thorax administered to the trancers by the various ministers are of this nature.

The kinetic event interrupting the dissociation is usually a single motion:

Luisa's mantilla slips from her head, and no one makes a move to adjust it. Finally she does it herself, and at this point the glossolalia utterance goes into Spanish while retaining the suprasegmental glossolalia pattern. A little while later she is back in glossolalia.

Or, as recorded about Lorenzo:

Lorenzo is rocking on his knees, hands on his thighs, but no glossolalia follows. He adds clapping, and glossolalia ensues. He throws up his arms, and the glossolalia is lost.

He prays, laying on his hands, and at the word *"poder"* he goes into glossolalia. Then he shakes the woman's head with both hands, and while doing so he loses the glossolalia.

Lorenzo, kneeling, places his hands on his knees, then sits back on his heels and straightens out alternately, quite fast. Or he simply rocks back and forth in the same position. He gets up, and his glossolalia ends simultaneously. Sometimes he straightens up and simultaneously raises his arms: at this point he goes into ordinary language. He places his hands in front of him on the floor and starts rocking back and forth. At this point he resumes his glossolalia. Even in this position, however, he occasionally returns to ordinary language.

Or:

Gilberto has his hands on his knees, rocking back and forth, uttering glossolalia. When he puts his hands on the edge of the podium, he lapses into ordinary language.

Ordinarily, this kind of interruption seems to come at the end of the utterance, at the point where it has already decayed. But especially when the arousal level is not very high, irregularities may be observed. About Lorenzo: "Occasionally a slip occurs: e.g., a glossolalia phrase breaks as he gets up from his crouched position before it ends, and he reverts to ordinary language."

This pattern may result in complete return to consciousness, i.e., wakening, which we want to take up in the next chapter.

6 Wakening

People do not remain in a state of dissociation indefinitely: after a while they return to an awareness of ordinary reality, they "wake up." The evolution of the vowel quality of the glossolalia utterances, from high-energy vowels to a *shwa* pattern, mentioned earlier, indicates what goes on: gradually or precipitously, the available energy becomes depleted, the dissociation weakens, the subject sighs, opens his eyes, and reverts to ordinary language. There are two factors, however, that interfere with this "natural" return to consciousness. There is the possibility of recovering the energy level, which then will lead the subject away, as it were, from the conscious state before completely reaching it, thus reverting once more to full dissociation. This process is very much like attempting to jump off a moving merry-go-round: it is easy when it slows down, but if you miss that point, around you go again until the next cycle of turns is completed.

The other factor involved is the quality of the dissociation: the more recently the behavior has been acquired, the harder it is to sense just when that jumping-off point might come around. Thus, the trancer needs help.

There are people who can provide their own help, their jumping-off signal. They will perform a single, often abrupt movement, and this will interrupt the dissociation. Gilberto will place his hands on the edge of the altar, and his glossolalia will stop. Lorenzo rises from his knees, and the dissociation is interrupted. As we have seen so often in other contexts, the mechanism may be effective even if not wanted under the particular circumstances:

135

Lorenzo now comes to Chela who has her paralyzed infant in her arms. He kneels down but does not succeed in going into glossolalia. Finally, he manages, but utters only a brief section. He wants to "take it over" to the child [praying in glossolalia over a patient is considered particularly curative], but as he gets up, he loses it almost immediately.

Perhaps the instruction for the mechanism is already taken along into the dissociation, and then cannot be nullified in the altered state.

There are others who need signals to be provided for them from the outside. All manner of stimuli may serve as such signals, and I would suggest that they probably vary from culture to culture. A pat on the back may do, or in the example of the congregation in Jalisco, where the trancers were beginning to undress, a beating with the pastor's belt. The most frequently used signal in the congregations observed is the ringing of a small, clear-toned bell with a very high pitch. The channel for external stimuli we spoke of earlier is open to this signal, probably by prior instruction. Again, *how* open the trancer is to the signal is a function of the time elapsed since the learning took place.

In the conscious state, Libet (1966) suggests that peripheral stimuli, no matter of what intensity, require about half a second to become consciously perceived. In light dissociation this reaction time is usually somewhat prolonged, perceived by the observer simply as a brief hesitation. Sometimes the interval will be longer: "Lorenzo sounds the bell. It takes Emilio more than five seconds to react to the signal." On occasion, a second signal may be needed: "Neither Francisca nor Emilio reacts to the bell: it takes a second ringing before they fade out."

Before genuine stereotypy has been established, the interval between signal and reaction to it may be even longer:

During the altar call, Anita goes into glossolalia, then does not pick up the signal for waking, and continues until the hymn sung after the altar call by the congregation, now back in their seats, is nearly completed.

How much the wakening is also a matter of learning is demonstrated by observations on subjects engaging in the behavior for the first time. Depending on individual differences, I have seen or received reports about the period of dissociation lasting from about fourteen hours to a whole year.[1] For instance, Consuelo told me, and this was confirmed by others in the congregation, that during the week-long prayer for the Holy Spirit in Mérida in July 1969,

a student of about eighteen cried through one entire
service, could not stop, then started vomiting. A doctor
was called, who gave him an injection [not specified].
His mother wanted him to stay home from the service the
next day, but he insisted on going. He went back into
crying during the prayer session, finally broke into
glossolalia, whereupon he stopped crying.

It is quite possible that not even the doctor's shot, perhaps a tranquilizer, completely restored the student's consciousness, and for this reason it was easy for him to lapse into the sobbing pattern of the previous night. The energy discharge of the vocalization then aided in the wakening.

The following is a detailed observation of the same pattern in the Mexico City congregation:

[Cuarta Iglesia, 17 June 1969. Prayer for the Holy
Spirit. Excerpt.] The service is being held in the former
dining hall of the church, very cramped quarters for the
approximately thirty-five adults present. Pastor Torres
is at the piano; there are two guitarists. One I know from
last year, the other one, Teófilo, is new. The young man
leading the service is also new, an enthusiastic Indian,
about twenty-eight, small, agile, very good oratory. After
the introductory hymn, he gives a brief sermon in which
he refers to the fact that the Lord greatly manifested
himself last Sunday and would surely manifest himself
again.
A *corito* is sung, very fast, with a strong rhythm.

[1] During light dissociation, eating, sleeping, and other normal
physiological functions continue, although sometimes with difficulty,
as evidenced by the case of Maria Luisa (see p. 39).

The deacon makes the congregation repeat its chorus
three times, and there is intense clapping. During the
subsequent repetition of the first verse, he motions for
the congregation to approach the rostrum for the first
altar call. Very quickly, one of the women and Teófilo
go into glossolalia. The key pulse, so familiar to me from
last year, at once emerges, but I also seem to detect some
different ones from Teófilo. I assume that he may be
one of those in whom the Holy Spirit has manifested itself
last Sunday, as mentioned in the deacon's sermon.
Teófilo shakes his head during his trance; the woman
glossolalist is down on knees and palms.

The deacon calls for testimony, and Teófilo tells,
somewhat incoherently, of being grateful for what the
Lord has done for him. If you ask, he will hear you, and
answer your prayer, he says several times. Incoherent
I am calling his statement only because he seems a bit
more repetitious than the other people giving testimonies,
and his voice sounds somewhat tense, as though he were
not quite out of his dissociation. I therefore focus my
attention on him.

The deacon reads from the Acts, the brief section about
the Pentacost. Then he calls for a very lively *corito*, "*Dios
está aquí, que precioso es . . .*," and the congregation falls
in with energetic clapping. During the singing, various
people start coming forward and kneeling down. Teófilo
places his guitar on the bench and kneels down. He soon
goes into very intense dissociation. He claps with
enormous rapidity, jumps on his knees about a foot
from the floor and sideways. His glossolalia is very loud,
and there are many others in it at the same time. The deacon
rings the bell, the glossolalia abates, but Teófilo does not
react. Torres goes to the piano in an obvious attempt
to get through to him, but there is no response. It is now
8:20. The deacon tries with repeated calls of "*Gloria a
Dios*," but again to no avail. So he asks the congregation
to start the *corito* once more, and for those who have not
yet received the Holy Spirit, to come forward. The
presence of the Holy Spirit, he says, will help them.
One boy kneels next to Teófilo, very close by, then two
women, then another late-teenage boy. The *corito* sends

Teófilo into an enormous recovery of his trance level,
but his utterance is not as long as before. Now, he bends
over, comes up again, clapping, shaking his head,
right hand up, left stiffly down, somewhat twisted back.
Then both his arms go up. He leans back against the
rostrum. All this time there is glossolalia, from him, and
from many others in the congregation all around me.
The boy next to Teófilo is doubled up, the deacon is
bending over him, pressing both his hands on his back
and shaking him very rapidly. The boy kneeling on the
left in the same row is also dissociated now, shaking his
head back and forth very fast, bending over, coming back
up repeatedly. Teófilo is still in trance with intermittent
glossolalia, practically collapsing on his knees. Sometimes
he has his arms extended outward and up, sometimes
he is on all fours.

A young man beside me is in very light trance, clutching
his hands tightly [not kneeling]. He shakes his head
continually, and his glossolalia is only a very light
$s \ldots s \ldots s \ldots$ To the right and a bit to the front of me
stands a girl; I know her from last year; she has her eyes
closed tightly, lifting herself up and down on her toes,
her heels not touching the ground. I put the microphone
close to her head; she notices nothing of it. Farther over
to the right a small, very old woman with a beautiful
old wrinkled face, completely toothless, is clapping furiously,
her eyes closed, obviously dissociated, but I cannot get
close enough to her with the microphone. Beside her,
another woman is also in trance.

Teófilo is now turned toward the rostrum, bending
down, now nearly collapsing against it, still uttering
glossolalia. The girl next to me opens her arms, holding
them slightly upward in the posture of benediction. She
is jumping up and down very fast, her toes not leaving
the ground.

Juan D. L. joins the congregation at this point and
starts praying over the boy on the right, by Teófilo. Torres
is bending over another one, listening to him.

8:55. Teófilo is still dissociated, with intermittent
glossolalia. Juan utters repeatedly, "*Gloria a Dios*," one
of the signals used to end a prayer session and for the

glossolalists to wake up. Torres joins in. But again, Teófilo
does not receive the message.

Some of the people begin to waken. The deacon takes
Teófilo's guitar in what seems to be an attempt to get
through to him. He intones the *corito*, "*Quédate, Señor. . . .*"
This produces another grand recovery of the glossolalia
level in Teófilo in terms of volume and intensity; he shakes
his head rapidly, opens his arms wide in the benediction
posture, keeping them high and rigid. The girl beside me
is clapping and jumping up and down. Her mantilla drops
to the floor. I pick it up and hand it to another woman
who places it on the girl's head. The mantilla is wet with
perspiration.

Teófilo's head is bent back; he is still in glossolalia.

9:05. No change in Teófilo; he still utters glossolalia,
now has another rise in energy level; occasionally, he
shakes his head. But his energy gradient is beginning to
slope downward, although he cannot wake up. The deacon
keeps calling out, "*Séllalo, Señor, séllalo, . . .*" Teófilo
tries to rise from his knees, falls back down on them,
attempts a recovery of the glossolalia, which is rather
weak. Juan, standing right next to him, now is also in
dissociation, in glossolalia, with exactly the same pulses
as last year, although with negligible intensity and volume.

9:10. Many people are quiet now. Teófilo is on knees
and palms. Juan, once more involved with the boy on the
right, is back in glossolalia, but his trance is rather brief.

9:15. A number of people are leaving. Teófilo has
another recovery; it is rather brief. He is weaving back
and forth on his knees. Finally he manages to get up,
leans against the rostrum, with a somewhat vacant look.
He utters an occasional single pulse, like an afterthought,
almost like a sigh. Fumblingly, he tries to brush the dust
from his knees.

Final benediction by Torres. Teófilo slips back into
dissociation, utters a few phrases. He wakes up, rubs
his eyes.

The offering is being taken up to another *corito*.
Teófilo picks up his guitar. He seems dazed. In a forlorn
fashion, he hunts through his pockets for the pick. The
corito sends him into another utterance: rather, it is just
a phrase, and soon, he starts playing his guitar.

Torres offers the final prayer, and Teófilo utters another phrase, like a comment.

After the service I stand in front of the benches to exchange greetings with the *hermanos* and *hermanas* who know me from last year, and who come up to shake hands. Juan brings Teófilo. He is dark-skinned, slender, and small, black hair, dressed in worn overalls. In a big-brother fashion Juan tells him to greet me. Teófilo does, shaking hands with me [his hands are neither hot nor sweaty!], saying, with just a bit of hesitation, "*Dios le bendiga.*"

"See," Juan says, patting him on the back, "you can do it. It's still a little hard, but you can speak Spanish now."

I understand from the subsequent discussion that this boy was "baptized by the Spirit" this past Sunday, and could not revert back to Spanish until Monday morning. So that first time he was dissociated for about fourteen hours. This time, he woke up after approximately seventy minutes. Torres has not seen another case like it, but he has heard of one where it took the person a week to recover his capacity to speak in ordinary language after receiving the Holy Spirit for the first time. "This person went about his daily chores, but could not speak Spanish."

There are cases of even more prolonged recovery, although they are probably rare. It will be recalled that Maria Luisa (p. 39) tells of a whole year's initial reaction to her first glossolalia experience. During that time, all the various signs of dissociation are present: tightness of the throat muscles (trouble ingesting food), vomiting, the daily compulsive slipping back into more intense levels with glossolalia, the perception of elevated body temperature during the night. She feels herself being "enclosed in a prison," a striking conceptualization of the altered state from which she cannot escape. It is not until the physician treats her for anemia that, most likely both because of medication and due to the waning energy level of her dissociation, she finds her way back into wakefulness.

High-energy, hyperarousal behavior, especially coupled with vocalization, is understandably interpreted by the uninitiated observer as abandoned emotionality. This is how, for example, contemporaries viewed the services held by John Wesley. It should be clear by now that what is impressionistically lumped together, part and parcel, as raging ecstasy is really behavior unfolding on many different levels of variously available energy resources. Excitement is not a primary factor but rather a contributing factor only. This is the point to be illustrated by the next observation.

I mentioned earlier that the small congregation of Utzpak, in the summer of 1970, was showing signs indicative of a "classical" revitalization movement. It was thought that the Second Coming was imminent, nightly vigils were held, men were sent on urgent evangelizing missions, visions were seen, and Satan was thought to possess one of the *hermanos* and had to be exorcized repeatedly. It was against this backdrop of high excitement and apprehension that the service of 30 July was held.

Violeta, fifteen at this time and holding the center of the stage, had had her first glossolalia experience on 7 September, 1969 and was just barely beginning to drop to the level of stereotypy. Higher levels of arousal were thus entirely available to her, and to my mind, the emotional climate of that week simply facilitated her going back to these levels. It is revealing that the following night, that is, the night after the service to be reported here, with tensions running just as high, she had her behavior under considerable control, just as Teófilo did at the Cuarta Iglesia in Mexico City two days after his first experience.

The following record from the field notes focuses on Violeta. Sections concerning the behavior of some of the other *hermanos* are edited out to some extent, as well as details of the service.

[Evening Service, 30 July 1970. Utzpak, Yucatán.]
People go into glosslalia almost instantly. Nesto is praying in glossolalia with outstretched arms, Floriano is perspiring profusely. Violeta is shaking, screaming, and sobbing at the altar, doubled over. Roberta has a similar sobbing pattern. [I hear this only from the teen-age girls and married women, never from the boys of the same age.]

Emilio is shouting out a prayer, still in ordinary language.
Neri's little girl is screaming. Chela has started praying
in glossolalia; now Emilio is in. Violeta continues at the
altar, and when Isaía, who is in charge of this part of the
service, rings, she cannot react. Francisca's tears are still
flowing, Anita does not react either, Luisa's glossolalia,
a very high "?*ai* ?*ai* ?*ai*," also continues. Isaía rings again;
still no response. A dog wanders in, sniffs at a dead bug
on the floor; no one pays any attention to him. [Such an
occurrence usually produces instant, indignant reactions.]

It is customary to go on with the service and to proceed
to the next section, even though some supplicants may still
be in glossolalia. Isaía tries to get hold of the situation
that way. He calls special hymns, and the first one to come
forward is Alfredo. He begins but is hardly audible above
the still very intense glossolalia of Violeta and Luisa.
Now the latter begins alternating between normal language
and glossolalia phrases, and Violeta has a richer pulse
inventory, showing that both are exhausting their energy
level. Lorenzo still has his back to us, kneeling on the
podium serving as altar, one hand on his hip. Alfredo's
usually loud singing cannot be heard. Anselmo is sitting
beside Vicente [who a bit earlier had been hallucinating]
in the front row of the men, shaking him by the neck:
Vicente has finally stopped shouting. There is much saliva
in front of Luisa, who is once more back in glossolalia.
Violeta is also still in. Lorenzo turns, throws a glance at
her, then continues with his prayer, once more facing
the wall. Luisa's dress is soaked with perspiration. Teresa,
Joaquina, and Francisca are also back in glossolalia.
Violeta throws up her arms, then continues rocking.
Vicente has become calm; he sits with his eyes closed,
his head slightly leaning back. Luisa has woken up,
is praying in ordinary language, but is still rocking on her
knees, and then goes back into glossolalia. Violeta continues
in dissociation. Alfredo has completed his hymn, and
Nacho and Nesto are offering one. Luisa seems to have
regained conscious control; she wipes her eyes, so does
Violeta. For the latter, waking is not complete, for in a
brief moment she is back in glossolalia.

Isaía announces Bible reading, and Luisa goes back

into glossolalia. There may be others—I can only
concentrate on the main actors—but there is a tremendous
din accompanying all of this. Lorenzo goes on praying.
Once more, Luisa wipes her eyes; Violeta is sobbing and
rocking, her glossolalia now is at the *"sə-sə-sə"* level of
near exhaustion. Luisa gets up and goes back to her seat,
Violeta continues with *"sə-sə-sə."*

A *corito* is called for, and the offering is gathered in,
while Luisa has briefly regained some consciousness,
only to lapse once more, even more strongly, into the
glossolalia pattern. Vicente is offering a special hymn,
and Violeta's kinetic pattern becomes very energetic;
her elbows are trembling, and she throws her trunk over
to one side, then the other; her rich pulse inventory is
audible in the pause before the general prayer is started.
She holds her head very rigid; her hands are closed, then
opened; she is rocking on her knees. Lorenzo, still on the
podium, lifts his arms. Violeta slips back into the
"sə-sə-sə" pattern.

Isaía passes to Lorenzo, who gets up and goes to the
rostrum. Violeta has lost most of her vocalization capacity,
is sighing rhythmically, *"ˀohhh, ˀohhh, ˀohhh."* Lorenzo
announces the biblical text to be read from the Acts,
but since Violeta continues, he bends down to her and
places his head on her head, which sends her into a brief
but very steep recovery of the trance level, after which
she has trouble swallowing. She is shaken by the rhythm
of the trance, struggles with the accumulating saliva,
obviously with very rigid throat muscles.

Her mother Chela, large with child, is now beside her,
trying to get her to wake up from the dissociation.
Lorenzo does not get to read his passage. There is a scene
developing between Martín and Anselmo. Violeta still
cannot swallow. Chela has her hand on her daughter's
shoulder, Violeta is sighing, ". . . *sí, Dios mío, sí, no
puedo* . . ." over and over again. Everybody is praying very
loudly; there is a terrific din, although just minutes ago
Lorenzo had asked for silent prayer. Chela has begun to
fan Violeta; she is back to a sighing pattern, still in
dissociation. Chela is handed a glass of water for her.
Vicente is asking for a prayer at the altar, and Violeta

is led, or rather half dragged, half supported, away from
the altar, to the first of the row of chairs in the juvenile
section, in the center. She does not sit; rather, her head
rests on the back of the chair, her outstretched legs on
the front edge of the seat. Both Chela and Eusebia are
now fanning her, while another glass of water is being
handed to them from the back. Anselmo is being possessed
by the Devil, and when he recovers he tells Lorenzo that
Satan has gone out into the street. He leads Lorenzo out
through the men's aisle, with most of the adult men behind
them. We hear very loud glossolalia from the outside,
which sends Violeta back into a recovery of her trance
level, as she half lies on the chair, her head rigidly back,
her hands stiff and hard looking. When she starts up,
first in real language, then in glossolalia, Francisca sobs
out and also goes into dissociation; so do all the other
women around. Two small brothers and three sisters of
Violeta, sitting on the children's bench beside me, are
sobbing in real distress. Isaía comes over to Violeta, in
glossolalia, his eyes tightly closed, then he goes back
to the table. Nina sinks on her knees beside Violeta,
in glossolalia; she collapses on her elbows and stays in
that position, very rigidly, her hands as stiffly graceful
as a Dresden figurine's, all through the rest of the service,
only occasionally rocking slightly. Roberta, another
fifteen-year-old, is also in very high glossolalia, getting
quite hoarse. Chela is crying over Violeta; she tells her
children to leave, but none of them—they are all still
sobbing—obey her. Some more water is passed down.
Violeta is sobbing out names—Marta, then the husband
of Reyes, then Nina—which are eagerly listened for and
passed on down toward the back of the church: the
Holy Spirit has voiced its dissatisfaction with them.

Lorenzo comes in from the outside, steps up to Violeta,
putting his hand on her head, telling her to control herself.
When she keeps repeating the same phrases over and over
again, sobbing, trembling, he says, "*Ya lo diste*,"—you've
already said that—"*ya lo diste*." Her chest is heaving.
He continues in soothing, but loud voice, "Sí, hija, sí,
hija,"—yes, daughter—while shaking her head lightly.
Roberta behind her screams out her glossolalia, very

much modeled on Violeta's, but without names. "God will
use you," Lorenzo tells Violeta, "Yes, he will. I know
about him [about Reyes' husband, who is considered
"*muy rebelde*," very obstinate in the matters of the Lord,
because he prefers *Hermano* Gruber's Baptist services
to those of the *Apostolicos*], I know already. Give her
water," then again to her, "*Sí, hija, sí . . .*"—yes, daughter,
yes.

Still, Violeta is not awake, and Chela with Lorenzo
takes her out to the back, into the *casa pastoral*. Nina says
next day, "Violeta was sick because the Spirit intoxicates
the person."

Complete wakening has easily discernible physical signs:

A moment ago, there was a flushed face, tense muscles,
profuse perspiration. Now there is pallor, for Lorenzo
with his light complexion more easily visible than for the
other parishioners, perspiration gone, demeanor calm,
all movements relaxed.

Or:

Finally Anita lapses into ordinary language, gathers up
her one-year-old son who has in the meantime crawled
up on the podium, and calmly goes back to her seat.
This is always so extraordinary to observe: the trembling,
shaking, sobbing, and then the total calm, not a trace of
it after waking, not even the eyes show any signs of crying,
as they most definitely would had there been weeping
in the awake state.

Sometimes, however, wakening is not complete. A platform of dissociation very close to consciousness is reached,
not by any means as rich in energy content or as intense in
dissociation as, for example, Maria Luisa's seems to have
been during that year following her first glossolalia, but
still discernible. The person may simply appear a bit dazed,
slow, perhaps sullen; especially memory and reactivity will
be somewhat inhibited.

[August 1969, Cuarta. Talk with Juan D. L. after service]
Juan says that attending the Bible Institute does not oblige

to any service in a congregation. But a deacon who wants
to become pastor has to serve a two-year test period.
"When is yours over?" I ask. Lots of hesitation, finally
he answers, "Next May . . . I think." "Where is Pastor
Torres?" "I think . . . I don't know . . . I think, Durango."
"What for, is there a pastors' meeting?" No idea, renewed
hesitation, guessing, about something that is always
much discussed and common knowledge in the entire
congregation. What's the matter with the young man?

Occasionally, both speech and motor behavior will be
affected while the subject speaks in ordinary language.

Anselmo, who when in the conscious state has a clipped,
rather fast delivery, is speaking as if in slow motion, with
each syllable drawn out.

[Later in the same service.] Anselmo comes marching
down the aisle between the men's and the juvenile section,
his trunk slanting slightly forward, right arm stiffly
upward, as if with a Roman salute, his legs apparently stiff
in the knees. With one finger, very rigidly, he points to the
mike. Lorenzo gives it to him, and he begins, with mounting
excitement shouting into it, his face flushed, eyes half
closed, then torn open as if by an outside agency,
perspiration dripping from his forehead. "Jehovah is with
us—Jehovah has said, six o'clock tomorrow morning.
He who forgets is not with Jehovah."
Lorenzo takes the mike: "This is Jehovah's message
for tomorrow."

It is in this type of residual, lingering dissociation that in
many congregations the so-called interpretation follows the
speaking in tongues. The Bible subsumes interpretation
under the gifts of the Holy Spirit. This classification, translated into our terms, would indicate that in the primitive
church it was clearly recognized that this is also a dissociative behavior.

Viewing the glossolalia behavior as a whole now, the
question is often asked what electrical brain wave patterns
accompany it. A great deal of work has been done in this
respect on hypoarousal dissociation, i.e., meditative trances,

by, for example, Hoenig (1968), Kamiya (1968), and R. K. Wallace (1970), to name just a few. They regularly encounter a stable α wave. No comparable data are available for hyperarousal dissociation. Inquiries sent to more than eighty colleagues in several fields turned up only one reference: Dr. Zaretsky, Princeton University Department of Anthropology, called my attention to an M.A. thesis done for Professor Luther Gerlach at the University of Minnesota by one of his students (Palmer 1966). In two of his five glossolalia subjects (examined in the laboratory, of course, which would probably have considerable effect on behavior) he found an increase in the heart rate and some changes in the brain-wave patterns (see Table 3). It is in the nature of things that the glossolalia behavior is considerably less amenable to scientific testing than is meditative dissociation, which is, of course, regrettable.

TABLE 3

ELECTROENCEPHALOGRAM AND PULSE RATE
OF GLOSSOLALISTS

		Subject F	Subject K
pulse		76 → 84	78 → 84
pulse		68 → 74	? → 90
EEG activity:			
α	frequency ↑		↓
α	amplitude ↓		↓
Θ	absent		present

After Palmer (1966).

Another question, asked with equal frequency, is that concerning glossolalia and meaningful utterance: could glossolalia not, after all, be some sort of language? There seems to be a psychological necessity to equate vocalization with speech, for what else could "speaking" be? Humans have an urgent need to understand what they experience, to explain new observations in terms of what they already know. They want to integrate that which is strange into a system of what is known and knowable. If they cannot do that, if "considering . . . two (cognitive elements) alone, the obverse of one element would follow from the other," says Festinger (1957:13), they experience cognitive dissonance. This, he maintains, produces tension and anxiety and needs to be resolved. Thus Mr. R. of London, after the unsettling experience of inadvertently vocalizing under the effect of LSD (see p. 124), came to the conclusion that he had somehow experienced man's early history—he had accidentally recreated the *Ursprache*, the original language of mankind.

In other instances the hearers may know that the glossolalist speaks no foreign language. Hearing him utter unintelligible discourse, they may then surmise that, possibly by supernatural intervention, he has now acquired this capability. As mentioned in the Introduction, they are convinced that they are listening to a living—or dead—language that could be understood if only someone were around who knew it. This way out of the cognitive dissonance produced in the listener by nonlanguage vocalization is termed xenoglossia (from Greek, a foreign tongue). When speaking of his own conversion experience, Gilberto, for instance, maintained: "All of a sudden I sang, and I spoke in Greek and Latin, and Chinese, and other languages I had never heard." Here are some examples from the literature:

When the day of Pentacost had come, they were all together in one place. And suddenly a sound came from heaven like the rush of a mighty wind, and it filled all the house where they were sitting. And there appeared to them tongues as of fire, distributed and resting on each one of them. And they were all filled with the Holy Spirit and began to speak in other tongues, as the Spirit gave them utterance. Now there were dwelling in Jerusalem Jews, devout men from every nation under heaven. And at this sound the multitude came together, and they were bewildered because each one heard them speaking in his own language (RSV. Acts 2:1–6).

[In religious ecstasy] Huguenot children of the late 17th century are said to have spoken correct French, which differed considerably from their native patois of the Cevennes Mountains (Cutten 1927:48–66).

Some years ago Tommy Hicks was in Russia.
Suddenly his interpreter left him. . . . Then he began
to speak in tongues and the Holy Spirit gave him the
language of the people to whom he was speaking (tract
distributed in the Streams of Power congregations).

Last week a woman arose during the [Pentecostal]
meeting and spoke for ten minutes, no one apparently
in the audience knowing what she said. An Indian who
had come from the Pawnee Reservation in the territory
that day to attend the services, stated that she was speaking
in the language of his tribe and that he could understand
every word of the testimony (Sherrill 1964:39).

Harald Bredesen, an ordained minister, went to a
mountain cabin and prayed around the clock, in order
to experience what in the New Testament is called the
Baptism of the Holy Spirit. He finally experienced the
most beautiful outpourings of vowels and consonants and
also some strange, guttural syllables. It was as if he was
listening to a foreign language. An old farmer of Polish
descent later said it was Polish. Sometime after this occurrence, he prayed in the presence of a young girl. The latter,
a student of Arabic, maintained that what she heard was
old Arabic (Sherrill 1964:13–14 and 15).

There are several reasons why belief in xenoglossia is
ubiquitous. First of all, there is a concrete basis for it: glossolalia shares with human speech certain universal char-
acteristics. It exhibits almost exclusively speech sounds, of
which there is only a limited inventory in the known languages of the world: man employs only a relatively small
number of those physiologically possible as speech sounds.
Also, glossolalia has an alternation of consonants and
vowels, and it has accent, pauses, final contours, intonation.
Purely as a matter of statistical probability, some conso-
nant-vowel combinations occurring in a glossolalia utterance
may also be a meaningful unit in some language. Thus,
[siø] could be French (old objective case of *sire*), [veni]
Latin. Word fragments might on occasion be swept over
into glossolalia, from Spanish *ven* (come) in the latter case,

or the former from the frequently repeated *séllame, séllame*.
Yet, just to demonstrate how complex matters can actually
be, Juan D. L.'s first and second phrases (Fig. 11) have
the identical vowel and intonation structure of the way he
utters *Gloria ti*. This "upbeat effect" is lost in latter utterances, and hardly appears again when in 1969 his stereotypy
has been fully established, so that we might theorize that
we are seeing something similar to the receding memory
function in the Umbanda variations on a melody fragment
washed over into the dissociation.

In addition to the above factors deriving from the sound
track, there is also operative a number of psychological
factors, I think. Foremost among them is the manner in
which people react to anomalous data, how they cope with
incongruities. In a psychological experiment carried out in
1949, J. S. Bruner and Leo Postman asked experimental
subjects to identify on short and controlled exposure a
series of playing cards. Many of the cards were normal, but
some were anomalous, that is, a red six of spades and a
black four of hearts. Soon all subjects identified all the cards
correctly, except that the anomalous cards were almost always, without apparent hesitation or puzzlement, identified
as normal. Listeners to tongue-speaking go through a similar process: they fit the audiosignal into a previously prepared category, namely language.

Finally, this type of approach is reinforced by social
needs. For Gilberto it is important to appear sophisticated
in worldly terms, for this is one of the requisites for a successful evangelist within the context of the present revitalization movement in Yucatán. Upon scrutiny, some of the
examples quoted earlier easily reveal similar motivations:
the Pawnee Indian alone in a white congregation, the Polish
farmer talking to a minister.

In summary, the answer to the xenoglossia belief is in
Chomskyan terms that glossolalia is not the surface structure of a linguistic, symbolic code, of a linguistic deep structure, but rather, in terms of the present research, an artifact

of hyperarousal dissociation. Or, we might say that glossolalia has for its deep structure the hyperarousal dissociation.

This brings up an important point, namely that of the structure of a mental state. Much of modern psychology concerns the structure of the conscious state. Freud was interested in that of the unconscious. Sleep research is also concerned with state structure. In examining hyperarousal dissociation, through the window, as it were, of glossolalia, we have also been trying to discover structure, to outline regularities.

Western man, as we know, is quite ambivalent toward dissociative behavior, being both fascinated and repulsed by it. One of the reasons for this ambivalence may well be that, to him, all seems chaos beyond the threshold of awareness. Committed as he is to control, to order, to the measurable, weighable, calculable part of reality, he may be even afraid to sleep and needs drugs to deaden his apprehension before sinking into an uncontrollable realm, into the uncharted depths of chaos. Yet, as we have seen, beyond the threshold of the conscious there is not disorder but structure. And if we see it but dimly now, "through a glass, darkly" this is not because it is so unsure in its outlines, but because we have, dully and in ignorance, just now begun to take a first glance at it.

7 Cultural Elaborations of Hyperarousal Dissociation

As I mentioned in the Introduction, various altered states of consciousness, among them hyperarousal dissociation, have a world-wide distribution, although, not all societies make use of the total behavior in all its phases. Rather, various groups ritualize, institutionalize, and thus elaborate only one or a few of its several aspects. Because of the great number of societies and ritual patterns involved, here we shall look at only a few examples. Anyone familiar with the ethnographic literature will be able to call up many more.

Thus, for instance, the Siberian shaman uses dissociation almost exclusively, with meaningful speech occasionally added, probably during low-level arousal, which is then understood to be possession: "Die Geister, so nimmt man an, sprechen durch den Schamanen zur Gemeinschaft, geben Jagdglück und Gesundheit" (Lommel 1965:68).[1] Shamanizing begins by the shaman placing himself into dissociation by monotonous sounds, drumbeats, rattling, and dancing. His soul is thought to go on a journey, during which he encounters various spirits while his body "lies there as if dead." Losing consciousness in a type of faint is often seen as a result of hyperarousal dissociation. That, actually, we are dealing with this type of altered state is evidenced by the fact that the shamans display considerable kinetic manifestations and, even after being restrained by leather thongs, some continue trembling and twitching.

[1] "It is assumed that the spirits speak through the shamans to the community, bringing luck in hunting and good health."

Einige Schamanen tanzen so wild, dass sie zuletzt
wie tot zusammensinken, andere geraten in eine so
heftige Ekstase, dass man sie zuletzt festhalten und
festbinden muss, was nur mit äusserster Kraftanstren-
gung mehreren Männern gelingt. Dann zittert und
zuckt der gefesselte Schamane oft eine lange Zeit und
sucht sich loszuwinden, bis ihm die Trommel entfällt
und er dann wohl stundenlang wie tot daliegt
[Lommel 1965:68].[2]

Visions often occur, especially when the altered state
is first initiated, as in the case of Salvador. Apparently the
initial stages are much less amenable to control than later
phases of hyperarousal dissociation, perhaps for physiological reasons. Therefore, visions remain individually based,
as do other types of hallucinations, including auditory ones.
Usually, they are incorporated into a belief system as a
unique experience of the founder and possibly of some
important followers. Mohammed represents an interesting
example. The following are quotations (in the translation
of A. Guillaume) from Ibn Isḥāq's biography of the prophet,
written barely a century after Mohammed's death (Isḥāq
died in 768 A.D.).

'A'isha [the prophet's wife] told him that when
Allah desired to honor Muhammad and have mercy
on him, the first sign of prophethood vouchsafed
to the apostle was true visions, resembling the
brightness of daybreak, which were shown to him
in his sleep. . . . She used to say, "The apostle's body
remained where it was but God removed his spirit
by night."
The revelations stopped for a time so that the apostle
of God was distressed and grieved. Then [the angel]
Gabriel brought him the Sūra of the Morning, in which

[2] "Some shamans dance so wildly that in the end they collapse as
if dead. Others are seized by such a violent ecstasy that they finally
must be restrained and tied up, which can only be done by several
men, exerting all their strength. The manacled shaman then often
trembles and twitches for a long time, until he drops his drum and
may then lie for hours, as if dead."

his Lord, who so honored him, swore that He had
not forsaken him, and did not hate him.

When it was the night on which God honored him
with his mission and showed mercy on His servant
thereby, Gabriel brought him the command of God.
"He came to me," said the apostle of God, "while
I was asleep, with a coverlet of brocade whereon was
some writing, and said, 'Read!' I said, 'What shall
I read?' He pressed me with it so tightly that I thought
it was death; then he let me go and said, 'Read!'
I said, 'What shall I read?' He pressed me with it again
so that I thought it was death; then he let me go and
said, 'Read!' I said, 'What shall I read?' He pressed
me with it the third time so that I thought it was death
and said, 'Read!' I said, 'What shall I read?'—and
this I said only to deliver myself from him lest he
should do the same to me again. He said,

'Read in the name of the Lord who created,
Who created man of blood coagulated,
Read! Thy Lord is the most beneficent,
Who taught by the pen,
Taught that which they know not unto men.'

So I read it, and he departed from me. . . . When
I was midway on the mountain, I heard a voice from
heaven saying, 'O Muhammad, thou art the apostle
of God and I am Gabriel.' I raised my head towards
heaven to see, and lo, Gabriel in the form of a man
with feet astride the horizon, saying, 'O Muhammad,
thou art the apostle of God and I am Gabriel.' I stood
gazing at him moving neither forward nor backward;
then I began to turn my face away from him, but
towards whatever region of the sky I looked, I saw him
as before."

. . . They said, "He is a Kāhin." He said, "By God,
he is not that, for he has not the unintelligent murmuring
and rhymed speech of the kāhin." "Then he is
possessed," they said. "No, he is not that," he said,
"we have seen possessed ones, and here is no choking,
spasmodic movements, and whispering."

The parallels to the behavior detailed in this investigation
are truly striking: Mohammed sees visions—only light in-

itially. Just as in the case of Salvador, there is a cessation of the experience, accompanied by anxiety. Since the subsequent visions show interpretable shapes (Gabriel), we may assume on the basis of hyperarousal dissociation that the intensity of the level is lower than at the beginning. Like Nina or Consuelo, Mohammed has difficulty distinguishing between visions and dream. In the latter he reports intense pressure on his chest, a diagnostic trait of hyperarousal dissociation.

The road from vision to other phases on the same continuum is open, as we have seen. Yet Mohammed chooses not to travel along that path. He is intent on religious innovation, and does not institutionalize dissociation behavior for the very reason that it *is* available in contemporary Arab culture. Both intense and low-level trance occur, the former with glossolalia ("choking, spasmodic movements, and whispering"). The low-level behavior is represented in the institution of the kāhin. This is the diviner of pre-Islamic times (Paret 1957) who, while possessed by a spirit familiar, gives advice on tribal matters such as war, but also on private problems, the location of lost camels, for instance. None of this is taken over into Islam.

As we have seen previously, vocalization is a secondary behavior, superimposed upon and evolving on the substratum of the dissociational state. If this view is correct, we may expect patterns other than vocalization to enter into this more or less tenuous relation with the altered state. This is in fact the case, and since, as we know, this aspect of hyperarousal dissociation, again probably for physiological reasons, is amenable to some control (in contrast to visions), a large number of different behaviors have been combined with the altered state and in this form institutionalized.

I mentioned the young woman who spontaneously started writing and drawing in trance (Goodman 1971b). In Bali, small girls are placed in dissociation and are then taught the vastly complex ritual dances (Belo 1960). Among the Wolof and Lebou in West Africa, dance is superimposed on the dissociation and the drummer literally drives the mentally ill subject into a peak and decay by accelerating drumming within the framework of curing rites (Zempleni 1966). The Shakers (Spiritual Baptists) have ritualized the kinetic behavior accompanying hyperarousal dissociation not as a dance but as rhythmic manifestation, which at its height assumes complete unison in breathing and in motion patterns, "so that [they] are depersonalized and unified [and] each person as if in a dance line, is reproducing the same movement" (Henney 1967:8).

Hyperarousal dissociation as a substratum of secondary behavior can be easily identified once the diagnostic traits are known. In the following instance a drama is played out in the altered state, and the excellent and complete observational data provide a good basis for analysis. (The authors themselves also offer one, which differs only in some details and in terminology from the one provided here.) The drama is a trance ritual from eastern Java, a dance with hobby horses plaited of bamboo, called *kuda kepang* (Darmadji and Pfeiffer 1969). The participants are boys of various ages; the manager is an older man, the *dalang*, reported to have magic powers.

a) *The Drama.* The presentation begins with a sacrifice of flowers, fruit, rice, an egg, and betel leaves. As he lights the incense, the *dalang* asks the *danjang* spirits to possess the players.

Four knights lose their way in the forest. They meet a monster hungry for human flesh, but they escape. He now tries to capture their clowning servant, who also manages to elude him.

The monster goes into a convulsive rage. Upon whispered instructions from the *dalang*, he turns into a wild boar, chomping on and consuming raw rice, tubers, and flowers. Uncontrolled raging and dance alternate, more or less under the control of the whispered instructions and the whip of the *dalang*.

The play concludes with a second attack of convulsive rage of the principal player. He sighs deeply, and with that the spirit leaves him and he falls asleep. (In other variants of the hobby horse dance the knights go into trance and eventually assume the role of their horses, eating straw, etc.)

b) *Dissociative Behavior*. The instructions carried into the dissociation are contained in the invocation, reinforcing what the players already know from being spectators of the play since earliest childhood:

> I am inviting you, Grandfather Danjang, Mother Danjang, Danjang Mintaraganarakusuma, Danjang of the prophets and the walis, Danjang of the four cardinal directions and the five principal places: your place is in the very middle. Come and assemble! When you have all assembled, I beg you show your miraculous powers and accord us your wisdom. Well then, let the play commence. But may it not harm or dismay the people. I beg you for your miraculous powers. Enter into the body of N. Take up your abode in the body of N. Do not leave until I grasp your hand and blow into N.'s ear. When you have left him, then may you all return, each one to his own place.

With the anticipation of possession, then, light dissociation sets in during the dancing and cavorting of the introductory scene. The dissociation deepens quite suddenly (when the player turns into a wild boar), and there are several peaks, drops of level, and recovery phases, similar to the evolution of the dissociation in glossolalia, and in this instance indicated by the alternation between response to the *dalang's* stage managing and uncoordinated raging.

There is a double signal for waking: the *dalang* whispers a command into the player's ear, and lightly taps his rigid muscles. Waking is not complete, though: although the muscles relax immediately, the player falls asleep and even when he wakes up, about half an hour later, he appears somewhat dazed and absent.

c) *Physiological Observations*. These are of particular importance to us, since for obvious reasons I could not carry out any of the tests mentioned here; but my observational data give ample circumstantial evidence that the same findings would be available from the glossolalists. Thus Darmadji and Pfeiffer found that the trancers did not react to pain (deep needle puncture) or to heat. Tapping the dorsal and volar side of the hand produced global stretch and bend reflexes. During the convulsive phase, intrinsic reflex action does not occur. After the decay of the trance, the reflexes remain somewhat more intense, but become normal, at the latest after the player wakes up from his sleep.

Blood pressure remains normal throughout. Pulse frequency increases to more than 100 during peak arousal; also, the depth and frequency of respiration rises. After wakening, pulse and breathing rapidly return to normal values. Because observers always stress the depressed hemorrhaging tendency during trance, the authors tested bleeding and clot retraction time, but found them both at normal levels.

There remains one more phase of hyperarousal dissociation: the residual trance, the state in which in Christian contexts the "interpretation" is produced. It has become the focus for ritual elaboration. Apparently, it represents a kind of platform phase (see p. 146 for a discussion of this phase) within dissociation, close to but not quite within the conscious level, which can be maintained for prolonged periods. Since it is still outside the conscious realm, sudden peaking can always occur, diagnostic of the presence of the hyperaroused state.

We have frequently referred to Umbanda. In this Brazilian curing cult the mediums are trained to stay within the low-level dissociation, conceptualizing the sudden "running away" of the behavior as unruliness of the possessing spirit that is mistreating its *cavalho*, its horse.

The platform phase, as it were, may be placed rather high, as we have seen in Anselmo proclaiming the will of Jehovah. It may be very low, as in the case of Juan in the fall of 1969. It may, on occasion, be evidenced mainly by certain

speech anomalies. Fitzgerald (1969) identifies through careful analysis of the prophetic speech of Ga (Africa) spirit
mediums the following trance-generated traits, which I have
arranged in a sequence going from low to high arousal:
— vowel elongation
— interruption or drowning out of speech
— interjection of sounds not employed in standard speech
— marked glottal constriction not normally occurring in
  similar environments
— hyperventilation, sudden volume increase and/or glottalization in initial positions of speech segments
— extremely high, suddenly rising pitch.
We need not again point to the marked cross-cultural agreements in this type of behavior.

Let us now come full circle and scrutinize once more
Malinowski's field observations about the *baloma*. We have
here a description of a low-level dissociative behavior engaged in within a religious context. The old man whom the
baloma possess is a respected member of the tribe. He is
not considered ill, and his encounter with the spirits is accepted as a matter of course. The presence of the dissociative state is indicated by a change in the quality of the
speaker's voice—a loud and high-pitched tone, and the
"fit" leaves him exhausted (marginally dissociated), causing
him to go to sleep afterward. And finally, the behavior
serves the ends of social control.

This brief review of a vast realm of human behavior is of
course in no way exhaustive; it does demonstrate, however,
some possibilities of ritualizing each of the many aspects
of hyperarousal dissociation.

We are coming to the end of our discussion. We have met
some groups of people and have seen how they enter into a
particular type of altered mental state, a hyperaroused dissociation. We considered how they superimpose their vocalization pattern upon this altered state and how they eventually return to the world of ordinary reality. There was
cross-cultural agreement in the emerging patterns, and there
was evidence that behavior other than vocalization could be

combined with the primary one of the dissociation. In every case, however, we found that the dissociation was the one that was patterning whatever was superimposed upon it, acting, as said earlier, as a nonlinguistic deep structure (in analogy to Chomsky's concept of the linguistic deep structure) for the surface behavior.

To my mind, we have barely touched the edge of a very large area of inquiry. As yet we know next to nothing about the physiological correlates of hyperarousal. We should examine the relation between religious concepts tied to the experience of this mental state and the neurophysiology of it. Glossolalia, perhaps, represents a window to otherwise hidden processes. We might ask, what happens to glossolalia and other speech behaviors when the hyperarousal is drug-induced, as is the case in many parts of the world?

Personally, I am most interested in the process of attenuation of the behavior. I want to know what happens, what time intervals are involved, how people cope with this experience, what consequences it might have on a personal and societal level. Others, I am sure, may have weightier questions as they think over what has been reported in these pages. I certainly hope so. Research if done well, I think, should be prologue.

Bibliography

Alland, Alexander
1961. Possession in a revivalist Negro church. *J. for the Scientific Study of Religion* 1:2

Allen, A. A.
1958. *I am Lucifer*. Revivals, Inc., Miracle Valley, Arizona. LP record No. 111.

Belo, Jane
1960. *Trance in Bali*. New York: Columbia University Press.

Benedetti, G.
1969. Das Unbewusste in neuropsychologischer Sicht. *Der Nervenarzt* 40:149–155.

Best, Elsdon
1925. *Tuhoe, the children of the mist*. vol. 1. (of 2 vols.) New Plymouth, New Zealand: Thomas Avery & Sons, Ltd.

Bloch-Hoell, N.
1964. *The Pentecostal movement: Its origin, development, and distinctive character*. London: Allen and Unwin.

Blair, W., and Refugio Vermont-Salas
1967. *Spoken (Yucatec) Maya*. Chicago: University of Chicago. Department of Anthropology.

Bourguignon, Erika
1954. Dreams and dream interpretation in Haiti. *American Anthropologist* 56:262–268.

1968a. Divination, transe et possession en Afrique Transsaharienne. In: *La Divination*, A. Caquot and M. Liebovici, eds. Paris: Presses Universitaires de France.

1968b. *A cross-cultural study of dissociational states*. Columbus: Ohio State University Research Foundation.

1968c. World distribution and patterns of possession states. In: *Trance and possession states*, Paymond Price, ed. Montreal: R. M. Bucke Memorial Society.

1970. Hallucination and trance: an anthropologist's perspective. In: *Origin and mechanisms of hallucinations*, Wolfram Keup., ed. New York, London: Plenum Press.

1971. Dreams and altered states of consciousness in anthropological research. In: *Psychological anthropology*, F. L. K. Hsu, ed., 2d ed. Homewood, Illinois: Dorsey Press, Inc.

Brumback, Carlos
1960. *¿Que quiere ser esto?* Springfield, Mo.: Editorial Vida.

Bruner, J. S., and Leo Postman
1949. On the perception of incongruity: a paradigm. *J. of Personality* 18:206–23.

Burdick, Donald W.
1969. *Tongues: to speak or not to speak.* Chicago: Moody Press.

Bryant, Ernest and Daniel O'Connell
1971. A phonemic analysis of nine samples of glossolalic speech. *Psychon. Sci.* 22:81–83.

Calley, Malcolm J. C.
1965. *God's people: West Indian Pentecostal sects in England.* Oxford University Press.

Chomsky, Noam.
1964. Current issues in linguistic theory. In: *The structure of language*, Jerry Fodor and Jerrold J. Kats. eds. Englewood Cliffs, New Jersey: Prentice-Hall, Inc.

Clark, Elmer T.
1934. *The small sects in America* (Revised 1949). New York: Abingdon-Cokesbury Press.

Cohn, Werner
1968. A movie of experimentally produced glossololia. *J. for the Scientific Study of Religion* 7:278.

Cutten, G. B.
1927. *Speaking with tongues: historically and psychologically considered.* New Haven: Yale University Press.

Darmadji, Tjiptono, and Wolfgang Pfeiffer
1969. Kuda Kepang—ein javanisches Trancespiel. *Selecta* No. 41:3283–90.

Diószegi, Vilmos
1958. *A sámánhit emlékei a magyar népi müveltségben.* Budapest: Akadémiai Kiadó.

Eliade, Mircea
1951. *Le chamanisme et les techniques archaiques de l'extase.* Paris: Payet.

Evans-Pritchard, E. E.
1965. *Theories of primitive religion*, Oxford: Clarendon Press.

Festinger, Leon
1957. *A theory of cognitive dissonance.* Evanston: Row, Peterson and Co.

Field, M. J.
1960. *Search for security: an ethnopsychiatric study of rural Ghana.* London: Faber and Faber

Fischer, Roland
1968. (with Philip A. Marks, Richard M. Hill, and Marsha A. Rockey). Personality structure as the main determinant of drug induced (model) psychoses. *Nature* 218 (No. 5138): 296–98.

1969a. The perception-hallucination continuum. A re-examination. *Diseases of the Nervous System* 30:161–71.

1969b. A biochemistry of behavior? *Biological Psychiatry* 1: 107–9.

Fitzgerald, Dale K.
1969. Prophetic speech in Ga spirit mediumship. Paper presented at the annual meeting of the American Anthropological Association, New Orleans, 21 November.

Fry, D. B.
1955. Duration and intensity as physical correlates of linguistic stress. *J. of the Acoustical Society of America* 27:765–68.

Gardner, Ernest
1963. *Fundamentals of neurology.* Philadelphia & London: W. B. Saunders.

Garrison, Vivian
nd. Marginal religion and psychosocial deviancy: a controlled comparison of Puerto Rican Pentecostals and Catholics. In: *Pragmatic religions: contemporary religious movements in America*, Irving I. Zaretsky and Mark P. Leone, eds. Princeton: Princeton University Press (in preparation).

Gaxiola, Maclovio L.
1964. *Historia de la Iglesia Apostólica de la fe en Cristo Jesus de México.* México, D. F.: Libreria Latinoamericana.

Goodman, Felicitas D.

1969a. Glossolalia: speaking in tongues in four cultural settings, *Confinia Psychiatrica* 12:113–29.

1969b. Phonetic analysis of glossolalia in four cultural settings. *J. for The Scientific Study of Religion* 8:227–39.

1971a. The acquisition of glossolalia behavior. *Semiotica* 3: 77–82.

1971b. Glossolalia and single-limb trance: some parallels, *Psychotherapy and Psychosomatics* 19:92–103.

1971c. Disturbances in the Apostolic church: case study of a trance-based upheaval in Yucatán. Unpublished Ph. D. dissertation, Ohio State University, Columbus, Ohio.

1972a. The Apostolics of Yucatán: a case study of a religious movement. In: *Religion, altered states of consciousness, and social change*, Erika Bourguignon, ed. Columbus: Ohio State University Press (in press).

Goodwin, Donald W., et al.

1969. Alcohol and recall: state-dependent effects in man. *Science* 163:1358–60.

Hall, Edward T.

1959. *The Silent Language*, Garden City: Doubleday & Co., Inc.

Hallowel, A. Irving

1948. Psychological leads for ethnological field workers. In: *Personal Character and Cultural Milieu*, D. G. Haring, ed. Syracuse: Syracuse University Press.

Haring, D. G. (ed.)

1948. *Personal Character and Cultural Milieu: A Collection of Readings*. Syracuse: Syracuse University Press.

Henney, Jeanette

1967. Trance behavior Among the Shakers of St. Vincent. Ohio State University Cross-Cultural Study of Dissociational States working paper No. 8.

1968. Spirit possession belief and trance behavior in a religious group in St. Vincent, British West Indies. Unpublished Ph. D. dissertation. Ohio State University, Columbus, Ohio.

Hess, Werner R.

1964. *The biology of the mind*, Translated by G. von Bonin. Chicago: University of Chicago Press.

Hine, Virginia H.
  1969. Pentecostal glossolalia: toward a functional interpretation. *J. for the Scientific Study of Religion* 8:212–26.

Hockett, Charles F.
  1958. *A course in modern linguistics*, New York: Macmillan.
  1964. (and Robert Ascher). The human revolution. *Current Anthropology* 5:135–68.

Hoenig, T.
  1968. Medical research on yoga. *Confinia Psychiatrica* 11: 69–89.

Isḥaq, Ibn
  1955. Sīrat Rasūl Allāh (The life of Mohammed) Translated by A. Guillaume, London, New York, Toronto: Oxford University Press.

Jaquith, James R.
  1967. Toward a typology of formal communicative behavior: glossolalia. *Anthropological Linguistics* 9 (No. 8): 1–8.

Kamiya, T.
  1968. Conscious control of brain waves. *Psychology Today* 1:56.

Kiev, Ari
  1964. The study of folk psychiatry. In: *Magic, faith and healing: studies in primitive psychiatry*, Ari Kiev, ed. Beverly Hills, Calif.: Glencoe Press.

Kleitman, Nathaniel
  1963. *Sleep and wakefulness*, rev. ed. Chicago: University of Chicago Press.

Koella, Werner P.
  1967. *Sleep*. Springfield, Ill.: Charles C. Thomas.

La Barre, Weston
  1970. *The ghost dance: the origins of religion*. Garden City, New York: Doubleday.
  1971. Materials for a history of studies of crisis cults. *Current Anthropology* 12:3–45.

Laffal, Julius
  1965. *Pathological and normal language*. New York: Atherton Press.
  1967. Language, consciousness, and experience. *Psychoanalytic Quarterly* 36:61–66.

Lalive d'Epinay, Christian
   1968. *El refugio de las masas*. Santiago, Chile: Editorial del
      Pacífico.

Lenneberg, Eric H.
   1967. *Biological foundations of language*. New York: John
      Wiley & Sons.

Lehiste, Ilse, and G. E. Peterson
   1959. Vowel amplitude and phonemic stress in American
      English, *J. of the Acoustical Society of America* 31:
      428–35.

Lévi-Strauss, Claude
   1963. *Totemism*. Translated by Rodney Needham. Boston:
      Beacon Press.

Libet, B.
   1966. Brain stimulation and the threshold of conscious ex-
      perience. In: *Brain and conscious*. J. C. Eccles, ed. Berlin,
      Heidelberg, New York: Springer Verlag.

Lommel, Andreas
   1965. *Die Welt der frühen Jäger: Medizinmänner, Schamanen,
      Künstler*. Munich: Callwey.

Ludwig, Arnold M.
   1968. Altered states of consciousness, In: *Trance and posses-
      sion states*. Raymond Prince, ed. Montreal: R. M.
      Bucke Memorial Society.

Mackie, A.
   1921. *The gift of tongues: a study in pathological aspects of
      Christianity*. New York: G. H. Doren.

Malinowski, Bronislaw
   1916. Baloma: the spirits of the dead in the Trobriand
      Islands; In: *Magic, science, and religion*. 1948. New
      York: Free Press (Macmillan).

Marks, Morton
   1969. Trance music and paradoxical communication. Paper
      read at the annual meeting of the American Anthro-
      pological Association, New Orleans, 19 November.

May, L. Carlyle
   1956. A survey of glossolalia and related phenomena in non-
      Christian religions. *American Anthropologist* 58:75–96.

Neher, Andrew
1961. Auditory driving observed with scalp electrodes in normal subjects. *Electroenceph. Clin., Neurophysiol.* 13:449–51.

Neher, Andrew
1962. A physiological explanation of unusual behavior in ceremonies involving drums. *Human Biology* 34 (No. 2): 151–61.

Othmer, Ekkehard, Mary P. Hayden, and Robert Segelbaum
1969. Encephalic cycles during sleep and wakefulness in humans: a 24-hour pattern. *Science* 164:447–49.

Palmer, Gary
1966. Trance and dissociation: a cross-cultural study in psychological physiology. M.A. thesis in anthropology, University of Minnesota.

Paret, Rudi
1957. *Mohammed und der Koran.* Stuttgart: Kohlhammer Verlag.

Pattison, E. Mansell
1968. Behavioral science research on the nature of glossolalia. *J. of the American Scientific Affiliation* 20:73–86.

Pfeiffer, W.
1968. Besessenheit, normal-psychologisch und pathologisch. Lecture delivered at the meeting on *Anthropologie der Ergriffenheit und Besessenheit* at Bad Homburg, Germany.

Pressel, Esther J.
1968. Structure, beliefs, and ritual behavior in Umbanda. Ohio State University Cross-Cultural Study of Dissociational States working paper No. 19.
1971. Umbanda in Saõ Paolo: religious innovation in a developing society. Unpublished Ph. D. dissertation. Ohio State University, Columbus, Ohio.

Prince, Raymond, Editor
1968. *Trance and possession states.* Montreal: R. M. Bucke Menorial Society.

Revival Movement "Streams of Power"
nd. *Life and life more abundant.* Baarn, Holland: Revival Movement "Streams of Power."

Sadler, A. W.
  1964. Glossolalia and possession: an appeal to the Episcopal Study Commission. *J. for the Scientific Study of Religion* 4:84–90.

Samarin, William T.
  1968. The linguisticality of glossolalia. *Hartford Quarterly* 8 (4):49–75.

Sapir, Edward
  1921. *Language*. New York: Harcourt, Brace & World, Inc.

Sargant, William
  1957. *The battle for the mind*. Garden City, New York: Doubleday.

Schafer, Ernest
  1950. Das Fest der weissen Schleier. Vieweg. c/c

Sherrill, John L.
  1964. *They speak with other tongues*. New York: McGraw-Hill.

Spoerri, Th.
  1967. Ekstatische Rede und Glossolalie. In: *Beiträge zur Ekstase*. Th. Spoerri, ed. Bibliotheca Psychiatrica et Neurologica No. 134. Basel: S. Karger.

Spoerri, Theodor
  1963. *Schall und Ton in der Medizin*. Munich: J. F. Lehmanns Verlag.

Stagg, Frank E., et al.
  1967. *Glossolalia*. Nashville: Abingdon Press.

Stoddard, I. C.
  1967. The effects of voluntarily controlled alveolar hyperventilation on CO_2 excretion. *Quart. J. Exp. Physiol.* 52: 369–81.

Suzuki, D. T.
  1960. Lectures on Zen Buddhism. In: *Zen Buddhism and psychoanalysis*. Erich Fromm, D. T. Suzuki, and Richard De Martino, eds. New York: Harper & Row.

Thompson, Richard F.
  1967. *Foundations of physiological psychology*. New York: Harper & Row.

Vivier van Etfeldt, L. M.
  1968. The glossolalic and his personality. In: *Beiträge zur Ekstase*. Theodor Spoerri, ed. Bibliotheca Psychiatrica et Neurologica No. 134. Basel: S. Karger.

Wallace, Anthony F. C.

1961. *Culture and personality.* New York: Random House. 2d ed. 1970.

1966. *Religion: an anthropological view.* New York: Random House.

1970. *Death and rebirth of the Seneca.* New York: Random House.

Wallace, Robert Keith

1970. Physiological effects of transcendental meditation. *Science* 167:1751–54.

Walter, V. J., and W. Grey Walter.

1949. The central effects of rhythmic sensory stimulation. *EEG Clin. Neurophysiol.* 1:57-86.

Wiechert, P., and G. Göllnitz.

1969. Stoffwechseluntersuchungen des cerebralen Anfalls-geschehens. *J. of Neurochemistry* 16:317–22.

Wierwille, Victor Paul

1962. *Receiving the holy spirit today.* New Knoxville, Ohio: The Way Inc.

Wolfram, Walter A.

1966. The sociolinguistics of glossolalia. Unpublished M.A. thesis, Hartford Seminary Foundation.

Worsley, Peter

1968. *The trumpet shall sound.* New York: Schocken.

Zempleni, A.

1966. La dimension thérapeutique du cult des rab. Ndöp, Tuuru et Samp, rite de possession chez les Lebou et les Wolof. *Psychopathologie africaine* 2:295–439.

List of Informants

Alfredo, 121, 142, 143
Anita, 65, 77, 81, 92, 136, 143, 146
Anselmo, 61, 72, 81, 82, 83, 95, 99, 130, 143, 144, 145, 147, 159

Chela, 28, 49, 50, 52, 63, 77, 136, 143, 144, 145, 146
Cilia, 95, 126
Consuelo, 61, 66, 137, 156

Emilio, 46, 48, 49, 63, 80, 81, 82, 121, 126, 130, 131, 132, 136, 143
Ermela, 45
Eusebia, 44, 68, 72, 80, 82, 89, 93, 145

Felipe (pastor), 51, 84
Floriano, 61, 64, 82, 93, 97, 142
Francisca, 63, 64, 77, 81, 97, 136, 143, 145

Gilberto, 41, 42, 43, 45, 52, 53, 54, 95, 126, 134, 135, 149, 151
Gregoria, 28, 52, 55, 88, 95, 128

Isaía, 22, 61, 64, 82, 95, 143, 144

Juan D. L., 14, 15, 28, 29, 30, 34, 35, 46, 49, 90, 95, 113, 114, 116, 117, 118, 119, 128, 132, 139, 140, 141, 146, 151, 159

Lorenzo, 18, 28, 40, 46, 65, 68, 71, 72, 73, 79, 80, 81, 82, 84, 85, 86, 87, 89, 92, 93, 95, 97, 99, 119, 120, 121, 126, 130, 131, 133, 134, 135, 136, 143, 144, 145, 146, 147
Luisa, 133, 143, 144, 145

Maria Luisa, 28, 37, 40, 46, 137, 146
Martín, 126, 129, 130, 144

Nacho, 130, 143
Nesto, 95, 142, 143
Nicolas, 49, 52, 55, 56, 63, 86, 88, 95
Nina, 45, 62, 145, 146, 156
Nohoč Felipe, 28, 44, 45, 46, 48, 58, 81, 82, 83, 93, 97

171

Subject Index

173